Nature

Design, &

Silk Ribbons

Nature

Design &

Silk Ribbons

Cathy Grafton

American Quilter's Society

P. O. Box 3290 • Paducah, KY 42002-3290

Located in Paducah, Kentucky, the American Quilter's Society (AQS), is dedicated to promoting the accomplishments of today's quilters. Through its publications and events, AQS strives to honor today's quiltmakers and their work – and inspire future creativity and innovation in quiltmaking.

Book Design – Jennifer A. Davis
Illustrations – Whitney Hopkins and Jennifer A. Davis
Cover Design – Karen Chiles and Jennifer A. Davis
Photography – Charles R. Lynch

Library of Congress Cataloging-in-Publication Data

Grafton, Cathy.
    Nature, design & silk ribbons / Cathy Grafton.
        p.   cm.
    Includes bibliographical references (p.).
    ISBN 0-89145-885-9
    1. Silk ribbon embroidery. 2. Appliqué. 3. Quilts. 4. Fancy
work. I. Title.
TT778.S64G73   1996
746.44—dc21

Additional copies of this book may be ordered from: American Quilter's Society, P.O. Box 3290, Paducah, KY 42002-3290 @ $18.95. Add $2.00 for postage & handling.

Printed in the U.S.A. by Image Graphics, Paducah, KY

Dedication

This book is dedicated to the memory of two special people in my life:

my mother, Barbara Zollinger, who taught me to love embroidery when I was seven;

and

my Nana, Lucille Cameron, who was always proud of everything I did.

Acknowledgments

There are many people who helped make this book possible. I thank them all for answering my questions and helping me in my hunt for antique silk ribbon embroidery pieces. Being able to prowl in the back rooms of museums and to see their treasures is almost reason enough to do research. My thanks to the Ohio Historical Society, Ellice Ronsheim, Jennifer Songster and Kim who showed me items from their collection; the Moravian Historical Society, Bethlehem, Pennsylvania, and Susan Schlack; the Kemerer Museum of Decorative Arts, Bethlehem, Pennsylvania, and Linda Robertson, conservator Dorothy McCoach; the Chester County Historical Society, West Chester, Pennsylvania, and Margaret Blades; the Hancock Shaker Village, Pittsfield, Massachusetts; Winterthur Museum, Winterthur, Delaware, Debrah Kraak, Gail in manuscripts, and my guide Mickey who showed me wonderful things.

I also wish to thank my family and good friends who gave me encouragement, ideas, and support or loaned me items for inclusion in the book. Thanks to Audrey Sanner; Maureen Carlson and Poplollies & Bellibones for the lovely shaded ribbons; Lillian Cagle, Peggy Hessling, Nancy Nielsen, Sandy Binyamin, Dee Ingles, Bruce and Linda Unterman, Joe and Mary Jobst, Dave and Omi Zollinger, Gaston and Klara Scheidegger, Sue and Steve Sanders, Tom and Molly Brown, Tasia Carr, Joane S. Lipinski, Diane DeRocher, Brenda Davie, Barb Lopez-Lucio; and to my afternoon quilt group for their encouragement. Special thanks to my husband, Maurie, and my children, Sarah, Tom and Kate, for their suggestions, proofreading, love and understanding while I took time to work on this project.

Finally, thanks to two people I have never met but who have greatly influenced me. Betty Ring has given us all a treasured legacy in chronicling our needlework heritage. Also, she made it easy to find the needlework she writes about by pinpointing museums and collection numbers. Jacqueline Enthoven fanned my imagination with a needle when I was in seventh grade. She wrote *The Stitches of Creative Embroidery*, which was the first hardback book I ever bought. I learned stitches and traveled the world as I turned those pages.

Contents

Chapter 1
INTRODUCTION 9

Chapter 2
**THE ELUSIVE HISTORY
OF SILK RIBBON
IN AMERICA** 13

Chapter 3
**SILK RIBBON, THREAD,
TOOLS, AND TIPS** 21
Silk characteristics 22
Silk ribbon 22
Silk thread 24
Novelty and metallic threads 24
Storage 25
Fabric choices for quilts embellished with silk
    ribbon 25
Hoops and hoop placement 26
Needles 26
Beginning – locking the ribbon on the needle 27
To knot or not to knot 29
Ending – knotting off 30
Controlling fraying and twisting of the ribbon ...30
Working smart 31

Chapter 4
**DESIGNING WITH SILK
RIBBON EMBROIDERY** 33
Introduction 34
Color 34
Silk ribbon colors and #99 ultramarine blue 35
Shaded ribbons 35
Inspiration and creativity 36
Design notebook 37
Getting started with designing 38
Finding your own design style 38
Variation versus replication 39
Dried flower designs 40
Marking your designs 42
Adding silk ribbon to your quilts 42
Silk ribbon and appliqué................................43
Silk ribbon and piecework 43
Silk ribbon on clothing 46

Chapter 5
THE STITCHES 49
Introduction 50
Stitch glossary 51
Flat stitches **52**
    Stem stitch 53
    Outline stitch 53
    Straight stitch..54
    Ribbon stitch (ribbon only) 54
    Cross stitch..55
Loop stitches **56**
    Alternating feather stitch............................57
    Single feather stitch 57
    Triple feather stitch 58
    Fly stitch..58

Extended fly stitch 58
Plume stitch (ribbon only) 59
Twisted plume stitch (ribbon only) 59
Knots **60**
French knot 61
Colonial knot..........................61
Coral stitch.............................62
Pistil stitch 63
Chain stitches **64**
Chain stitch 65
Whipped chain stitch 65
Detached chain stitch (lazy daisy) 66
Filled lazy daisy 66
Detached twisted chain stitch 67
Split stitch 67

COMBINATION STITCHES **68**
Spider web rose...........................70
Buds (rose and other) 71
Leaves and the calyx 73
Grapes, berries, and clumps 74
Feather stitch ferns 75
Baby's breath filler 76
Coneflowers 77
Dandelions and fly stitch flowers 77
Snowdrops and hanging flowers 78
Grasses and sedges 79
Feathers, fur, and hair 83
Facial features 84
Ruffles and flourishes – couched bows and
   ribbons........................85
Fans and medallions 86
Spider webs and spiders 88

Chapter 6
BUILDING A STRAND 89

Introduction 90
How to build a strand using silk ribbon and thread
Step 1 – Feather stitch base....................90
Step 2 – Detached twisted chain stitch leaves 91
Step 3 – Ribbon stitch leaves 91
Step 4 – Detached twisted chain stitch flowers ...91
Step 5 – Accent flowers 91

Step 6 – Final embellishments 92
Step 7 – Couched bow..................92
Variations 92

Chapter 7
PRACTICE PROJECTS 93

Colonial pocket 94
18th Century housewife (sewing kit) 98

Chapter 8
SILK RIBBON SAMPLERS AND SMALL QUILTS 103

Introduction 104
Quilting your samplers.....................104
Hanging your samplers 105
Sewing notions 107
Holidays – Hanukkah and Christmas 107
Friendship – Dee's Cocina 111
Pieced sampler – Crazy quilt runner 113
Family crest – Grafton Family 117
Celebrations – Dave and Omi's Huis 121
Appliqué sampler – Shaker Wreath 124
Appliqué quilt – Wildflower Basket 130

SOURCES AND SUPPLIES ...140

BIBLIOGRAPHY 142

ABOUT THE AUTHOR 143

Chapter 1

INTRODUCTION

Silk Ribbon Embroidery. Cathy Grafton.

I have been aware of the power of embellishment on quilts ever since 1982 when I saw a quilt called "The Floor of the Mosque." Rhoda Cohen designed this quilt to look like an oriental carpet, and she had sewn coin offerings on the surface. Rhoda later explained they were actually subway tokens, but they looked sufficiently exotic to me. I never forgot those coins gleaming here and there on the quilt and how much that embellishment added to the image she created.

In quiltmaking for the past few years there has been a growing interest in all types of embellishment. One form it has taken is some of the wonderful machine embroidery on quilts and clothing. Another direction is a personal favorite – dimensional appliqué which gives a quilt depth and richness with fabric and embroidered details. Found objects, buttons and beads, all used in many types of embroidery for years, are showing up with great regularity on quilts and quilted clothing.

Now silk ribbon embellishment is finding its own niche in the quilter's world of embellishment styles. Silk ribbon has gone from an unknown, almost lost art, to increased popularity very quickly. I think it offers a wonderful way to embellish quilts, clothing, and wallhangings. What I find so appealing about embellishment with silk ribbon is the natural look it gives to leaves, flowers, grasses, and even weeds. Because the silk drapes so well, petals and leaves look real and even whimsical fantasy flowers look like something you could pick right out of the garden. While silk ribbon embroidery looks complicated, it is really quite easy, and beautiful results can be achieved even by beginners. As you work, the flowers appear quickly, which makes it fun to do.

I got started several years ago after I read Judith Montano's first book on crazy quilting. While thumbing through it, a single line caught my eye – it mentioned that silk ribbon could be used to embellish crazy quilts. I had been looking for some way to expand my use of embroidery to add details to a quilt in progress and the idea of using silk ribbon stayed in my head.

I asked all my favorite quilt store shopkeepers if they had any silk ribbon and one of them sold me some out of her own small stash. I found that it was just the right scale to add background details to my dimensional appliqué, and I immediately began to explore other ways to use this wonderful ribbon in my quilts.

Combining silk ribbon embroidery with appliqué is my special area of interest and one that I feel has only begun to be explored by quilters. Clothing is also a wonderful place to experiment with types of embellishment, and silk ribbon offers great possibilities here also. And of course, we quilters can create a whole new generation of crazy quilts emblazoned with silk ribbon and threads.

The interest in embellishment is growing and, as the availability of silk ribbon continues to increase, I foresee that quilters everywhere will embrace this option for embellishing their quilts. I see many possibilities for combining silk ribbon and quiltmaking each time I work. Here are a few.

▶ Combined with appliqué to add detail and richness to the overall design
▶ On crazy quilts – a definite star in embellishment techniques
▶ On quilt borders of all kinds to add touches of color and texture
▶ Creating details in pictorial quilts
▶ Gracing vests, jackets, bridalwear, holiday, and children's clothing
▶ On wallhangings, small banners, and pieced ornaments
▶ With touches of lace for a Victorian look on almost anything
▶ On stuffed animals and doll clothing

I encourage you to find your own style when embroidering with silk ribbon. Some of the work I have seen is very dainty and petite and some has a Victorian look. I work on a slightly larger scale which I find complements my appliqué. It could also be done in other styles, such as art deco with sharp angles and stylized stitches. There are many books which can give you ideas on styles and designs once you learn to work with the ribbon. The embroidery tradition is full of rich and varied stitches, many of which can be worked with silk ribbon.

As you experiment with silk ribbon and threads, you will find favorite combinations of stitches which you can use over and over again. Many of the flowers I make use very basic embroidery stitches, but by setting them in different ways and using wonderful colors, they look new and fresh each time I create them.

Silk ribbon will be a wonderful addition to your appliquéd and pieced quilts. Whether you use silk ribbon embroidery as the main focus of your quilt, or as an accent, you will see that it adds another dimension of detail, texture, color, grace, and beauty.

In this book we'll explore silk ribbon history; discuss how to create your own designs, including designing from nature; learn stitches and techniques; and try some small projects and samplers that will introduce you to silk ribbon embroidery. With a little practice you can have the skills to add this unique form of embellishment to your own work.

Notes & Sketches

Chapter 2

THE ELUSIVE HISTORY OF SILK RIBBON IN AMERICA

"Everything was embroidered. The tender downy head of the newly born baby was covered with a cap of delicatest material encrusted to hardness with needlework... A large part of the 18th and the first quarter of the 19th Century was a period of remarkable skill in all kinds of stitchery."

Catherine Wheeler – *The Development of Embroidery in America*

To learn about the history of silk ribbon embroidery, I first did lots of reading. I immersed myself in books about embroidery and social history of the eighteenth and early nineteenth centuries to try to get a feel for where silk ribbon fit into the stitchery of the time. Then I traveled to the eastern United States to visit museums and historic sites where I could study some early pieces of silk ribbon embroidery.

Embroidery was an important part of eighteenth century life in America. Women attending the earliest "dame schools" sometimes focused primarily on sewing arts. After the American Revolution, numerous female academies sprang up throughout the eastern United States where young girls continued to learn sewing, mending, and embroidery as a part of their education, along with a greater emphasis on reading and writing. Until the Industrial Revolution in the 1830s, home sewing was just that and familiarity with sewing skills was considered an essential part of a young girl's preparation for life. Personal items were embroidered for many reasons – to mark and keep count of linens, to show the maker's status, and certainly, consciously or not, embroidery was an important form of artistic expression for women. Fashions in types of needlework came and went. Visitors from Europe brought the latest styles which were learned and then taught here in America.

Young girls in school completed embroidered samplers under the careful direction of their teachers. These were often framed, presented to their families, and then hung in homes as examples of their daughters' skills. Regional styles of embroidery are sometimes traceable to the ethnic backgrounds of the various groups which settled here. In many cases, samplers show the style of a particular school or of the teacher who was most likely the designer of the work students produced. Books and engravings were early sources teachers used to help design samplers. Certain images were often repeated with

variations. Often a combination of techniques, including embroidery, painted details, bead work and bangles, could all be found on a single piece. Any painted backgrounds and facial features were usually done by the teacher. School accounting records show payments from students to teachers for prepping their samplers' painted backgrounds.

Silk ribbon itself was first used in America to border samplers during the last quarter of the eighteenth and on into the nineteenth century. Some of these ribbon "frames" were sewn down flat with mitered corners or rosettes of ribbon attached on the corners. On others, the ribbon was gathered and then sewn down in a serpentine fashion, sometimes with intertwining gathered bands of fabric.

Silk ribbon embroidery appeared in French needlework during the mid-1700s; however, tracing its development in America is not easy. It was a widely used decorative style in the French Court on clothing and accessories, and from there passed to other areas of Europe, including England and her colonies. From my readings, I also know that silk ribbon embroidery had spread to the German states and Saxony, and it is from this area that I believe silk ribbon embroidery came to America in the 1800s.

Ads from Philadelphia newspapers in the last quarter of the eighteenth century, just after the American Revolution, describe many types of fancy and unusual needlework which were taught, but make no mention of silk ribbon work. The lack of examples of silk ribbon embroidery in museums and no mention in books from that time period lead me to believe that the Moravians were the first to introduce silk ribbon embroidery to America. Embroidery experts Betty Ring and Susan Burrows Swan also believe the Moravian schools were the first to introduce silk ribbon embroidery in America.

Advertisement for Linden Hall Seminary for Young Ladies. Lititz, Lancaster Co., Pennsylvania.
Courtesy, The Winterthur Library: Joseph Downs Collection of Manuscripts and Printed Ephemera. Winterthur, Delaware.

Crazy quilt. Ohio Historical Society, Columbus, Ohio. Circa 1884.

Detail of broom with silk ribbon and chenille flowers.

Embroidered sampler with silk ribbon border. Mary Caley, 1837.
Chester County Historical Society, West Chester, Pennsylvania.
Photo credit: George J. Fistrovich.

Kemmerer wreath. Silk ribbon, chenille, chiffon flowers. Mary Ritter, 1824.
Kemmerer Museum of Decorative Arts, Bethlehem, Pennsylvania.

The Moravians were a religious group, followers of John Huss, which originated in an area of the modern day Czech Republic. They were persecuted for their religious beliefs and eventually found refuge on the Saxony estates of Baron Zinzendorf who became their patron and protector. They established settlements in America, the best known ones in Bethlehem, Pennsylvania, and Salem, North Carolina.

Soon after they arrived in America, they established a Young Ladies Seminary in 1742 at Germantown, Pennsylvania, which was later moved to Bethlehem. In 1746 a female academy, now Linden Hall, was established in Lititz, Pennsylvania. With the establishment of these two schools and also an academy in Salem, North Carolina, the Moravians demonstrated their commitment to education for women at a time when women had few educational opportunities.

Kathleen Eagen Johnson, in her thesis on Moravian culture, "To Expand the Mind and Embellish Society," mentions that silk ribbon embroidery pieces were bought over from the Herrnhut (the main Moravian settlement in Saxony) in 1818. This is the earliest reference to silk ribbon embroidery in any of my reading. Moravian school records show that charges for silk ribbon began to appear that same year on students' accounts. She also notes that in 1829 ribbon work was being taught by a "German lady."

By the mid 1820s, silk ribbon embroidery was considered a part of the needlework fashion of the day. In 1826 the students at the Bethlehem Seminary created a floral presentation wreath for First Lady Mrs. John Quincy Adams. It was done in silk ribbon, chenille, and silk chiffon. She wrote them a delightful letter of thanks and kept the wreath even after returning to private life.

Advertisements for the Bethlehem Academy mention ribbon work as one of the many types of embroidery taught, along with ebony work, worsted (Berlin) work, painting on velvet, and crepe and chenille work. In my travels to Bethlehem and the Henry Francis DuPont Museum in Winterthur, Delaware, I saw examples of silk ribbon embroidery worked on decorative framed wreaths, smaller items such as needlecases and silk twill bags, and several beautiful longer, unframed embroidered panels. Many of the ribbons were delicately shaded and appeared to be in excellent condition. The stitches on these pieces are the traditional silk ribbon embroidery stitches we use today. All the pieces are estimated to date from the first half of the nineteenth century.

Even among the Moravians where we know silk ribbon embroidery was taught along with other needle arts, music and academics, there was little evidence to show how large a role it had played in the needlework development of the young ladies. Almost all the silk ribbon work that I saw included other forms of embroidery as well. Chenille, silk chiffon (known as crepe work) and bead work were common accompaniments to the silk ribbon. Spangles and small silver ornaments were often added to the framed pieces. I believe that silk ribbon was a minor style in the embroidery heritage of early America. Museum collections have just a few examples of it here and there and, very little seems to have been written about this technique.

Silk ribbon embroidery passed in and out of popularity throughout the rest of the nineteenth century, most often being used to decorate accessories. It was also referred to as "China ribbon" embroidery and as a form of rococo embroidery. Probably the strongest revival was during the last decades of the nineteenth century for embellishing crazy quilts. In the early twentieth century there was some ribbon work done on clothing and accessories, but much of that was done with manipulation of the ribbon rather than embroidering with it.

Today the strong work of Australian and New Zealand embroiderers has once again brought silk ribbon embroidery to public attention. Silk ribbon is becoming widely available in stores and is being taught in America more than ever

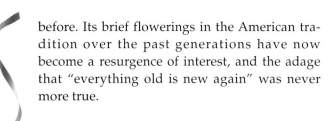

before. Its brief flowerings in the American tradition over the past generations have now become a resurgence of interest, and the adage that "everything old is new again" was never more true.

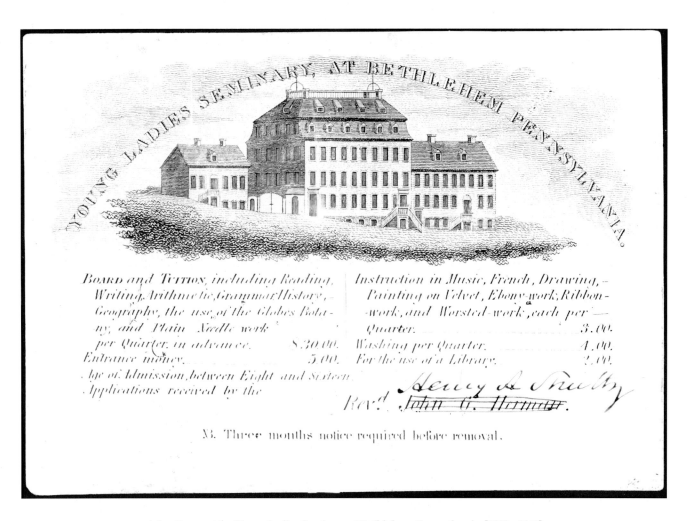

Advertisement for Young Ladies Seminary at Bethlehem, Pennsylvania. [1840 – 1849]
Courtesy, The Winterthur Library: Joseph Downs Collection of Manuscripts and Printed Ephemera. Winterthur, Delaware.

ABOVE: Crazy quilt with silk ribbon embroidery. Collection of Sandy Binyamin, Clarendon Hills, Illinois.
BELOW: Details of Crazy quilt with silk ribbon embroidery.

Chapter 3

SILK RIBBON, THREAD, TOOLS, AND TIPS

"Silk is a unique fiber: in how it looks, in how it feels and, for the textile artist, in how it works."

Cheryl Kolander – *A Silk Worker's Notebook*

In this chapter you will learn about the materials and tools you will need to do silk ribbon embroidery. I have also included tips and techniques for working with silk ribbon and basic instructions for beginning, knotting, and ending.

Some people have a hard time believing that silk ribbon is used the same way as thread and that it does indeed pass through the material in most stitches. Many times I find people looking at my work trying to figure out how the silk stays in place. They cannot believe that it is stitched through the material.

SILK CHARACTERISTICS

Silk is a wonderful fiber – both strong and delicate at the same time. Silk is known for being colorfast and for its resistance to fading. Silk takes on vibrant colors and has a luster that will make those colors dance in your work. Silk feels luxurious. It is also warm to wear and durable under most conditions.

Unfortunately, often we see old silks that have badly deteriorated. From the latter part of the nineteenth century through the early years of the twentieth century, silk fabrics were treated with heavy metal salts to create stiffness and a rich rustle dictated by fashion. These are the silks that we see shredded in old clothing and on turn-of-the-century crazy quilts. Since the salt process was only used for a short time, that type of deterioration is no longer a problem. However, it has left many people with the mistaken notion that silk is too fragile a fabric to use in handwork.

Most silks, including silk ribbon, can be washed if treated carefully. Silk should be washed in lukewarm water, never hot, with a non-alkali soap, such as Ivory. Use a delicate cycle on the washer to wash silk ribbon work or do it by hand. I prefer to dry the work by laying it flat instead of using a dryer. If you use a dryer, use the delicate setting (low heat) and do not overdry the work. If you must press the piece, try not to press directly onto the stitching which will flatten it out. Use a pressing cloth or terry towel under your work and the correct (silk or low) setting on your iron. Most silk ribbon embroidery pieces will not need frequent washing. If you are planning silk ribbon on clothing, use tighter stitches firmly secured to help it look good through many washings.

For the quilter, using silk ribbon may be a new experience and there are a few points to keep in mind. Because silk is strong yet delicate at the same time, you must take some care not to snag the ribbon. You will want to be sure that your hands are not too rough since they are the most likely cause of snags. I use a good, non-greasy hand cream regularly when working with the ribbon. There are several brands that you can find at sewing stores or by catalog which leave no residue on your hands; but any good quality cream will help. Or you can convince your family that they must take over dishwashing so that your hands will stay soft for your silk working. The ribbon can fray as you work and I will have some tips later on keeping that to a minimum.

SILK RIBBON

Silk weaving, including the making of silk ribbon, was encouraged under the reign of the French King Louis XIV in the first half of the eighteenth century. The area around Lyon, France, became a center for ribbon weaving and the ribbon produced there was used extensively at the French court to embellish court clothing. Later in the nineteenth century, silk ribbon embroidery was sometimes called "Chinese ribbon work." However, that doesn't necessarily mean that ribbon was imported from China – it may be just a name given to make it sound exotic. After the American Revolutionary War as trade to America opened up again, silk ribbon was imported in greater amounts than ever before. Today, however, almost all the silk ribbon we use comes from Japan, but is manufactured in China.

In this book when I speak of ribbon I will be talking about silk ribbon. There are also synthetic ribbons available, and you may certainly try them if you wish. I have found that they do not compare well to the feel and drape of pure silk ribbon. Silk ribbon is somewhat more expensive than the synthetics, but I feel it is well worth it. Before I located actual silk ribbon, I tried satin ribbon which required a set of pliers to pull it through all but a loose weave fabric. Nor did it drape like silk to create the natural looking flowers which give such charm to this form of embroidery. Since the focus of this book is silk ribbon, I will leave the synthetics to others for their experimentation.

Silk ribbon is most commonly found in three widths: 2 mm, 4 mm, and 7 mm. The 2 mm is just less than 1/16" wide and is very delicate. Using it is similar to using a heavy thread or pearl cotton. I like to use 2 mm for very delicate work, but I do not use it very often. I much prefer 4 mm silk ribbon which is about 1/8" wide and is widely available. Most stores carry it in the widest range of colors, and it is more affordable than the 7 mm. I like the scale of embroidery with 4 mm ribbon and find that it works well with appliqué. The 7 mm is just over 1/4" wide, and I use it to make larger flowers and leaves. I find it works well as an accent, although usually it cannot be found in as wide an array of colors as the 4 mm ribbon. There are larger widths available through some stores or catalogs; however, these are more often used to form flowers which are then attached, rather than for embroidery.

To start, I suggest collecting a good selection of 4 mm ribbon and perhaps a few accent colors in 7

mm. Since the 4 mm scale goes well with both appliqué and pieced work, you may find that is mainly what you want to use. I often suggest to students in my classes that they go ribbon shopping with a friend and each buy a good assortment of colors, including lots of greens if they will be working on flowers. Then they can go home and split each packet in half to double the colors each has. This is an economical way to get a good assortment of colors. Remember, you may have been buying fabric for 10 or 15 years just to get all the colors you want. So expect to take a little time to build up a good color array of silk ribbon. It is worth noting how much easier it is to slip a small bag of ribbon into the house unnoticed then several bolts of fabric.

Some stores and catalogs sell silk ribbon on five yard reels. Sources that specialize in silk ribbon may sell it by the yard and also offer hand-dyed or variegated silk ribbon. This was called shaded silk ribbon in the nineteenth century and gives an added dimension of naturalness to the colors of flowers and leaves. I still find an occasional quilt shop that sells only precut one-yard pieces, but this is the most expensive way to buy your silk ribbon. The ribbon goes quickly and you will soon find that you have favorite colors that you always want to keep on hand. Silk ribbon is now more available at some of the larger chain craft and sewing stores. See the Sources and Supplies section at the end of the book for specific suggestions.

Ribbon colors are coded by number. You can order color charts which show all the colors listed by number. I keep my own chart of favorite colors and look for those colors when I go to stores. If you order by catalog, you will usually have the broadest choice of colors. I find having my own color chart is invaluable in planning my work and in replenishing my ribbon supply.

SILK THREAD

Most stores and catalogs which offer silk ribbon also sell silk thread. It comes in a variety of styles and is excellent to combine with silk ribbon. Small details on flowers, stems, and grasses can all be done with silk thread. Specialty embroidery shops will give you the best selection. Quilt shops may only have one or two types of silk thread since it is a sideline product. The sheen of silk thread adds greatly to the visual effect of appliqué and pieced work, and I like to keep an assortment of textures and colors of silk thread. Probably best known is silk twist or buttonhole twist. This is a strong plied cord of silk thread which gives your stitches a cabled texture. It is easy to find and a good mainstay for your sewing basket. You will also want to try some softer flosses which have a half-twist and more body. A third type of silk thread is platte or "flat" silk which spreads slightly as you stitch. The platte silk has a beautiful luster, but will snag easily since it has little or no twist. There many other types of silk threads. Some are thicker or have softer or harder finishes, all of which affect the final look of your work. Try experimenting with ones that interest you. I have bought threads from China, Germany, Switzerland, England, and France and find working with them all exciting.

Silk is also processed for knitting and crocheting. You may want to investigate some of these thicker silks which have more strands. I divide one or more strands to get the thickness I desire and then use them for embellishment as I would other silk threads.

Silk thread can be somewhat slippery to use. Your stitches sometimes will loosen before they are secured. Make sure to hold enough tension as you sew each stitch until the next stitch is made.

NOVELTY AND METALLIC THREADS

Most of the time I prefer using silk threads rather than synthetics. However, I sometimes like to use different threads to produce certain effects. Pearl cotton comes in various sizes and colors and gives a thicker, slightly fuzzy line. It absorbs the light rather than reflecting it like silk, which makes a pleasing contrast when I am working grasses. I also have some linen threads which have soft, natural-looking colors and add a different type of texture to my work. Besides these natural fibers, you may want to try some of the many rayon and other man-made threads used for all types of embroidery.

Check out stores that specialize in embroidery materials or those that offer a good choice of synthetics. Ask the store clerks for help if you feel overwhelmed by the choices. It is good to have some sort of idea what you want to use these novelty threads for when you go to choose them. For example, I add spider webs to my quilts as a sort of signature – I like to use a silver metallic thread for them. Another time I went looking for something glitzy to make legs on a fabric appliqué heron and found a rough textured bronze rayon with just the right sparkle for the idea I had in my head.

Metallic threads will add some sparkle to your work, but remember that they can be a challenge. Using short lengths of these threads will help you to control them. I use them sparingly as an accent color or to add texture to my work.

STORAGE

It is important to find the best way to store your ribbon. I use baskets and Shaker boxes for storing my silk ribbon and silk threads, because I like to leave them out in my home where I do most of my embroidering on quilts. I store the ribbon by color in different baskets, so I can quickly inventory a basket to choose colors or to see what colors I need to replace.

Choose a storage system that works for you personally. I love my little boxes and antique baskets. I know that they are not as practical as see-through plastic boxes, but they fit well into my own decor, so I don't mind. A system of stacking plastic boxes provides a quick view of the available colors without having to open each box. Another way to store silk ribbon and threads is in drawers with dividers. This keeps the colors grouped and also helps to keep loose pieces of ribbon from becoming too tangled. I like to have a special place to store leftover pieces – this is my silk ribbon "scrap basket" which often yields the perfect accent ribbon when I need just one more touch of color.

Group by color, and then perhaps by size if you use several sizes in quantity. The threads will probably need their own storage containers and, of course, you will need a place for needles and other sewing notions. Think about where you sew and how much organization you want. The more ribbon you have, the more important it is to have a good storage system. It can be quite frustrating to know that you have some #36 green you need to finish a piece, but not to be able to locate it.

I find that as I near the end of a reel of silk ribbon, it is easier to take the last few feet off and store the piece in one of my boxes rather than trying to keep it wound on the reel. However, one advantage to keeping it on the reel is having the color number printed on the reel so you can be sure which color you are using.

FABRIC CHOICES FOR QUILTS EMBELLISHED WITH SILK RIBBON

The background materials that you choose will play an important part in how your quilt, sampler, or clothing looks. I like to use silk ribbon on a variety of fabrics and have found it works well on all of them. I often use it on a regular weave cotton cloth and for embellishing pieced or appliqué quilt tops. I also like the look of silk ribbon on linen or raw (noil) silk. I have not had any undue problems passing the ribbon through these fabrics. The size of your needle probably has more to do with getting the ribbon through with a minimum of fraying than does the weave of the fabric.

You will want to do most of your silk ribbon embroidery on solid, mottled, or softly printed backgrounds. The ribbon work may disappear into prints with lots of contrast or which are busy with strong patterns. Very large prints may be of such different scale that the ribbon won't blend in a satisfactory manner. Dark fabrics allow you to use white, cream, and pale silk ribbon colors effectively.

Lately I have seen several varieties of open weave cloth sold for use with silk ribbon. I don't find it easier or necessary to use; silk ribbon works beautifully on even finely woven fabric. Sometimes the cloth is so coarse that it detracts from the ribbon designs.

For pieced work, especially on crazy quilts, you will be stitching through the seams. You can still embroider on any kind of fabric – just be sure your needle is large enough if you're working on tightly woven fabric, and take a little extra care when pulling the ribbon through seam allowances.

For appliqué work I choose the fabric colors first and then choose my silk ribbon colors. The ribbon can work as a color accent to the appliqué or, by using a similar color, can echo the fabric colors.

HOOPS AND HOOP PLACEMENT

In most cases, you will want to do silk ribbon embroidery on a hoop . A hoop helps to hold the fabric taut and keep the tension even. I suggest that you use a fairly small hoop, about 6" in diameter. With this size hoop you can reach into the center to manipulate the ribbon as you form your stitches, but you must reposition the hoop if your work extends over a larger area. Plan your stitching, working from the middle of the piece outward to avoid putting the hoop over areas you have already stitched. If you must move your hoop over completed stitches, try these tips to minimize distortion or crushing the ribbon.

- ▶ Open the top part of the hoop wide enough so you don't have to force it down over the fabric and the lower part of the hoop.
- ▶ Position the material so that any large flowers, such as roses, are not directly on the edge where the top hoop will be tightened.
- ▶ Tighten the hoop carefully, just enough to make the material taut, without over-tightening.
- ▶ Take your work out of the hoop when you aren't working on it.

Use the best hoops you can find. There are many on the market today and you can experiment to find out which you like best. I prefer nicely fin-

ished antique hoops and the finished screw-tightened wooden hoops that are imported from Germany and are available at many quilt and needlework shops. Spring-tension hoops can work, if they are of good quality. Certainly a 69¢ hoop from your local dime store will work, but the better made hoops hold the fabric tighter with even tension. The finished wood also feels nice in your hands.

You may also want to try working on a small frame. I have a scroll frame which holds a rectangular section of my work taut while I am stitching. I can then release the tension to roll my work as I move on to each section. These frames come in several styles and are available at good needlework shops, some quilt shops and through catalogs. (See Sources and Supplies.)

NEEDLES

A chenille needle is the best needle for silk ribbon embroidery. A chenille needle has a long eye, is sharp, and helps minimize fraying of the ribbon. The ribbon will go through your fabric, no matter what type of needle you use, but you need a needle which makes a large enough hole so that the silk will not become tattered as it is pulled through the fabric. Start with a size 20 chenille needle (they come in sizes 18-24). Your ribbon will probably still fray as you reach the end of a piece. I try to work on the more visible stitches with fresh pieces of ribbon.

At times you may also use a blunt tapestry needle for weaving the ribbon, such as for a spider web rose. When working with silk threads, use an embroidery needle. They come in many sizes. Pick one that you can thread comfortably.

For some special stitches, such as loop stitches, a trolley needle helps keep the ribbon in place until you stitch it down. A trolley needle is a ready-made tool which is available at some quilt stores, embroidery shops, and through stitching catalogs. It is nothing more than a steel guitar finger pick with a tapestry or heavy duty needle glued to the end. My husband plays guitar so we have plenty of finger picks at our house and I can make a trolley needle anytime.

Wear a trolley needle on the index finger of your non-sewing hand with the open end on the nail side (see illustration). This is handy because you don't have to set it down and pick it up, but like any new tool, it will feel awkward at first. If you can't locate a trolley needle or do not have any musicians in the family, you can use a toothpick, crochet hook, knitting needle, or your thumb to help you with these stitches.

You will often have ribbon, which you can use later, left on the needle. I suggest keeping a special pin cushion or needle case just for chenille needles threaded with these short lengths of ribbon.

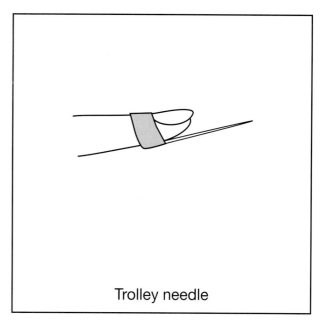

Trolley needle

BEGINNING – Locking the Ribbon on the Needle

The first thing you must know is the unique method of securing silk ribbon onto your needle. This is often known as a needle eye lock technique. The advantage to this method is that you can use the ribbon up to the very end of each piece. Start with a fairly short piece of ribbon – 12" to 14" in length.

1. First thread the ribbon through the needle. Because you are using a chenille or other large-eyed needle, this should be quite easy. Now pierce the ribbon with the point of the needle about ¼" from the threaded end (Step 1).

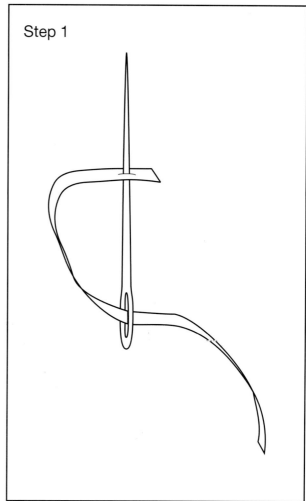

Step 1

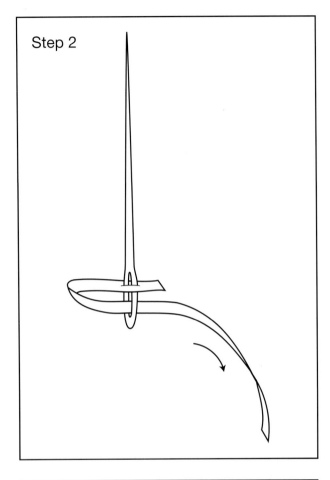

Step 2

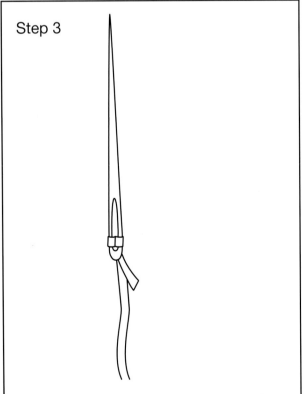

Step 3

2. You now have a small loop of ribbon which passes through the eye and a long tail of ribbon. Hold the point of the needle in the air so that it looks like the illustration at left (Step 2).

3. Now gently pull the longer tail of the ribbon, which will then lock the threaded end of the ribbon onto the eye of the needle (Step 3).

You are ready to stitch! The chapter on stitching will get you started with instructions for individual stitches and combinations. With a little practice, you can create your own combinations and explore some of the many other stitches which are part of the legacy left to us by countless stitchers from the past.

TO KNOT OR NOT TO KNOT?

Some people who work with silk ribbon use no knots. They use a separate piece of thread to tie off the ribbon or just weave it into the stitches on the back of the work. This does reduce clutter on the back of the piece and may help it to lie flatter. However, I use knots and don't find that they are a problem if I move them aside with my finger to avoid stitching through them.

One way to make knots with your silk ribbon is to wrap the ribbon around the needle three times and then slide the loops down the length of the ribbon to its end. This method is often used to knot thread.

Another way to make a knot is to take the end of your ribbon and pierce it about ¼" from the end and pull the needle through. Then catch the end loop with your needle like the illustration on the right.

Now pull the loop tight onto the needle and slide the knot down the length of the ribbon. Before this second loop disappears, slip your needle into it again and pull the loop tight onto the needle. Then slide this knot down the length of the ribbon. This knot will not overly stress the ribbon and after practicing a few times, you should be able to do this technique easily.

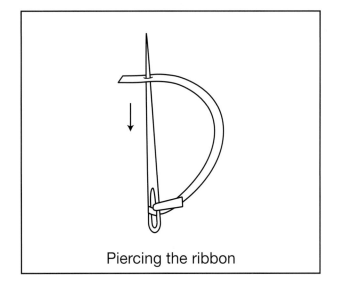

Piercing the ribbon

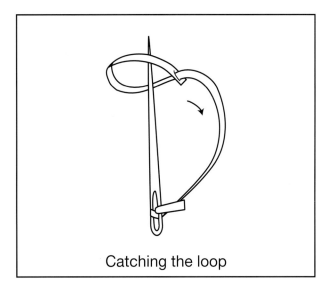

Catching the loop

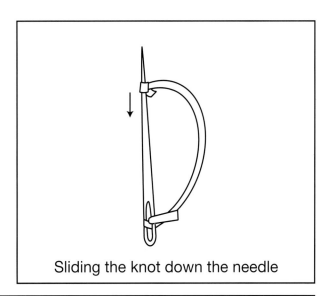

Sliding the knot down the needle

ENDING – Knotting Off

To end your ribbon, go to the back of the embroidery piece and slip your needle through the nearest ribbon. Catch the loop and pull tight as you would end any thread. Clip the ribbon ½" or so away from the knot.

Because you lock the ribbon onto your needle, you will discover you don't have any leeway for getting extra ribbon as you sew. If you are like most of us, you will also find that you tend to use up the ribbon until you have just a very small bit left with which to knot off or end. I have found myself in this situation so many times that I developed a way to knot off a very short ribbon.

You need at least enough ribbon to get your needle to the back of your work. Then stitch under the nearest bit of ribbon you can reach. If the ribbon is too short to do this, make the stitch using the eye of the needle instead of the point. Then as you slip the eye under the ribbon, turn it, and insert it through the loop you just made.

At times you may not have enough ribbon left to get the needle all the way through the loop. If this happens, push the eye through the loop and cut the ribbon right at the eye of the needle

which leaves as much tail of the ribbon as possible. Then remove the needle and pull the tail to tighten the knot.

When you are finished knotting off, unlock the ribbon from the needle by cutting it off with sharp scissors.

CONTROLLING FRAYING AND TWISTING OF THE RIBBON

Because silk ribbon is delicate, the constant rubbing against the fabric as the ribbon passes through will cause it eventually to fray. The best way to control this is to use a big enough needle and short lengths of ribbon, about 12" to 14". It will seem short to you at first, but try it and you will find that the stitches are easier to work and the ribbon will fray less. If the stitches are very visible flat stitches, use a fresh piece of ribbon. Use ribbon that is a bit worn for twisted stitches which will not show the wear like the flat ones.

When you first work with the ribbon, you will also find that it tends to twist. It is important to untwist the ribbon while making flat stitches. It is easier to adjust a stitch before you finish it than it is to go back and try to untwist it later.

Practice using your fingers to help guide the ribbon the way you want it to go – lightly hold the ribbon in place. I often use my left thumb. You may find another finger works better. At first it will seem awkward to hold a hoop, guide the ribbon and sew it down all at once, but your fingers will become accustomed to working with the ribbon very quickly, just as they did when you learned to quilt, piece, and appliqué. You can also use your needle to smooth out the ribbon if it becomes twisted or starts to curl. Hold the ribbon in your left hand and run the needle under the

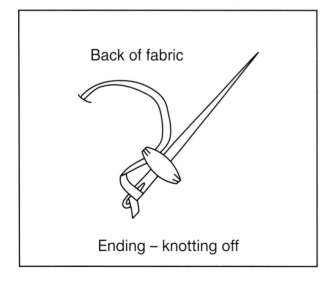

Back of fabric

Ending – knotting off

ribbon, back to the point where it comes out of the material.

There are many stitches which make good use of the twist and make realistic looking flowers. You can try some of those first if you have trouble, and save the more exacting stitches until you feel a little more experienced at working the ribbon.

WORKING SMART

By working smart I mean heeding a few common sense suggestions which can really make a difference in your stitching environment.

First, be sure that you have good lighting in all your work areas, especially where you do your embroidery. I have a small light that shines over my shoulder when I work. So often when blending ribbon colors, good light makes the difference between choosing glowing or garish color combinations. Silk ribbon reflects light and gives a subtle sheen to your work which is very appealing. You need to be sure of how the colors are blending for shading flowers.

Stretch often. Your neck muscles will get tired when you do handwork. You need to get up and move around every 15 minutes or half hour. Time seems to pass quickly when I sit down to sew and I often forget to stretch. If you get up, you will feel better and also give your hands a rest from repetitive movements.

Keep your work and sewing tools together and ready to go. When you have a few minutes to sew and have everything together, you are likely to use your time better. If, however, each time you must first go find your ribbon basket, something to work on, scissors, and a needle and those half-glasses for close work that you sometimes need (just to thread the needles), you are more

likely to do something else. My work is always ready and even if I only have 10 minutes, I can make good use of that time.

Use good tools! I find that over my years of quilt-making it is more important than ever to use well made, sturdy tools in my work. My first quilt frame was a rickety affair bought before I ever knew how to put a stitch on a quilt. It certainly worked, and I made quilts on it for over five years. However, when my husband built me a cherry sawhorse frame that sits rock solid on any surface, I found I no longer faced the small frustrations of using a poor quality frame. My quilting time became more enjoyable and relaxing.

You will find the same to be true with your silk ribbon embellishment tools. Tools are an important investment. Each time I buy a new pair of scissors I am reminded of this. I use scissors in the style of the different time periods of quilting and silk ribbon embroidery that I teach, so I have some wonderful antique looking scissors. I enjoy using them all the time for their sharpness and design. Small details do make a difference and using good scissors, hoops, and cloth will give you a finer sense and feel for the work you are doing.

Notes & Sketches

Chapter 4

DESIGNING WITH
SILK RIBBON
EMBROIDERY

"Look at the world – reflect
in your art the world as you
see it."

Nan Fairbrother – *An English Year*

INTRODUCTION

In this chapter I will teach you how to design in silk ribbon embroidery, whether you choose to create your own original designs or to practice your embellishment skills on some of the projects in the last two chapters of this book. I start with some personal observations about color and how to use it with silk ribbon to create the look of the natural world. Then I offer some thoughts on inspiration and creativity and some concrete ways to help you take ideas and turn them into the designs you want to make. I discuss specific ways to combine silk ribbon with quilts, using some of my own work as illustration. Finally, I have included some work of friends to show you how silk ribbon can enhance both handmade and ready-made clothing.

COLOR

Color is an essential part of design, often what we notice first in a work of art. I will give you some general suggestions on working with color, and then some specific advice on working with color in silk ribbons.

There are many wonderful books and articles on the market on color, but I prefer to make most of my own color choices directly from nature. This has come from years of observation and working to improve my sense of color. This isn't to say that I don't sometimes have trouble with color choices or that I don't continue to learn all I can about how colors work together. I have just been able to teach myself to look at nature to analyze the colors I see and how they work together.

Here are a few simple suggestions that you can try to develop your own color sense. First, each time you attend a quilt show or watch "show and tell" at a guild meeting, spend a few moments looking at each of the quilts just for their colors. Note to yourself what you like about the color choices on a quilt or what doesn't appeal to you or seem to work. At a show pick out several quilts that really "zing" with color, mark them on your program, ask yourself a few basic questions about the color in those quilts and jot down your thoughts to review later. Include notes on questions such as:

- ► Why are the color choices on this quilt so appealing?
- ► Are the color choices "safe"? Bold? Calming?
- ► Has this quilter chosen a primary, pastel, muddy, muted, or bright palette?
- ► What "surprise" colors has this quilter chosen?
- ► How has this quilter used color to help convey the design ideas in this quilt?

You can develop your own questions about color as well, but these are some to start with. Your goal will be eventually to train yourself to notice color wherever you are.

Second, try to look at nature with a color sensitive eye. When you look at flowers, trees, fields, and parks, spend a few moments thinking about the colors you see. Note the bits of accent colors, and if a landscape is particularly appealing, try to figure out what blend of colors makes it interesting. Try to get a sense of how the colors you are seeing work together. Ask yourself questions like these:

- ► How many shades of green do I see?
- ► Are they bright, soft, gray-green, yellow-green, etc.?
- ► Which flower colors seem to accent and which dominate?

- What kind of flower colors do I prefer - bright, pastel, muted, dark?
- What colors surprise me here?

Again, other questions will occur to you as well. I try to look at all kinds of scenes in my environment for a brief color analysis – as I walk down a city street, in a backyard garden, on a snowy day, or almost anywhere that I have a few moments to reflect on the colors around me.

Recently I was lucky enough to attend the Claude Monet exhibit at Chicago's Art Institute, and I studied several paintings in this way. Two absolutely new things hit me about color. One was Monet's treatment of snow. There were pinks, blues, and yellows in profusion as part of the snow. Blues and grays I expected, but the other "surprise" colors added sparkle and depth to the snow scenes. I found the colors intriguing and will use them when next working on a snowy scene. Second, I suddenly noticed Monet's use of bright kelly greens along with grayed and muted greens in the same nature landscapes. I always tend to use one or the other, but rarely blend them together. However, he had used them both and they worked beautifully.

By training yourself to be attuned to color wherever you see it and by studying nature, you will begin to instinctively understand what colors work in your own designs, and you will become more confident in your color choices.

SILK RIBBON COLORS AND # 99 ULTRAMARINE BLUE

A few words on color and silk ribbon. The palette of silk ribbon colors is quite extensive with over 200 colors. Since color is so vital to creating quilts that sing, choosing your ribbon colors will be an important consideration.

Some colors are so important as accent colors that I memorize them. I think the most wonderful one is #99, ultramarine blue, which I describe as electric blue. This color is vibrant and touches of it will add appeal and life to your work. Last year my husband and I visited churches and cathedrals in Switzerland and the Netherlands. I saw this exact shade of blue in the stained glass windows of each church we visited, from small village churches to grand city cathedrals. Sometimes it dominated the window for an extremely dramatic effect. Other times it was used as an accent, a strong color which caught your eye and said "look here."

There are several other colors which evoke feelings for me, such as warm and sunny #16 yellow orange, #50 dark wine red which gives a sense of velvety flower petals, and #86 purple black which has a dark intensity with just a touch of color. Spend some time discovering the ribbon colors that please you most and make an effort to keep them on hand so that you have plenty to choose from. Use a variety of them in your quilts and watch them sing with color.

SHADED RIBBONS

In the past silk ribbon came in variegated colors called "shaded ribbons." Embroiderers knew that using these shaded ribbons added another dimension of naturalism to their work as leaves and flowers in nature change color due to light, the age of the flower, and natural color gradations. Today you can find hand-dyed shaded ribbons from many sources and by adding some of these ribbons to the commercially dyed ribbons, you, too, can enhance your own designs.

Here are a few suggestions for using shaded ribbons. First, try using a shaded ribbon when you will be repeating a stitch, such as in a strand of ferns. Using close stitches of the ribbon shows the gradual change of color. If you use the shaded ribbon in stitches too far apart, it may look as if you are using different ribbons instead of the subtle color changes of shaded ribbon which suggest the play of light and shadow. Choose a shaded ribbon by picking the most dominant color – foliage colors for leaves and ferns and flower colors for blossoms, petals, and even whole flowers. Feel free to experiment, but in most cases, you will want to use a little here and a little there rather than basing the design exclusively on shaded ribbons.

Leaves and flowers are not the only good use for shaded ribbons. Use them in any place where you wish to add several colors in a subtle way. For example, you can add highlights to hair with shaded ribbon which would be difficult to plan out if you were changing ribbons as you went. Fur on animals and feathers on birds can also have extra dimensions of movement and depth when worked in shaded ribbons.

INSPIRATION AND CREATIVITY

Your design sense helps you personalize your work. For example, because stitching styles vary greatly from person to person, rarely do any silk ribbon designs look exactly the same. And since silk ribbon designs are often built up layer by layer, you can easily create or adapt a design by changing a stitch, color, or placement of stems, leaves, and flowers. As you develop your design sense, you will become aware of how your own

style works. Design can be as simple as making your own choices from many possibilities.

Inspiration is the part of design that comes from observing elements of your world and then using your imagination to translate an idea into a quilt. As the quote at the beginning of this chapter says, "Look at the world – reflect in your art the world as you see it." I believe that we create to show others how the world appears through our own eyes and that reflecting that vision through quilts (or paintings or whatever your creative outlet) is a desire that comes from within. Tasia Carr, a master embroiderer, says that "art is about that which has meaning." Art then is the expression of your own feelings and thoughts. We all see the world in our own way and have something to add to the body of general art. Remember that each creation does not have to be a masterpiece. Think of the simple geometric Amish quilts that are now considered art, although the makers probably intended only to make warm quilts for their families with patterns and colors that pleased them.

I think we as quilters need to encourage each other to express our own designs. We certainly have the technical skills. Those of you who have been quilting for years know such a range of techniques. Some people feel an urge to branch out into personal design work earlier than others, but it does come for most of us. In teaching over the years I have often heard quilters say, "I could never come up with the ideas to design a quilt," and with their next breath they say, "but I have always wanted to make a quilt about..." and go on to describe an idea that would make a great quilt. Often it is a fully formed idea, just waiting for the next step.

We all admire the work of quiltmakers who create their own designs and we may think that they have a gift that we don't have. While for some people original design work may be instinctive, most designers work hard to develop a design sense and are often inspired from other sources.

For example, when a painter paints a scene from nature, the finished product may look abstract, impressionistic, or quite different from the actual scene, due to her own design sense. Designers develop methods to translate their ideas into a quilt. Silk ribbon, with its smaller size and versatility, is an excellent choice for beginning to design your own work. You can learn and practice skills which will help you turn your ideas into something lovely made of cloth and silk ribbon.

In my own work I don't seem to lack for ideas and have often wondered where some of my ideas originate. Since I love nature, most of my quilts are based on a natural or rural scene. I often reflect the beauty and harmony that I see, rather than an actual place. The constantly changing rural America that I know is a bittersweet place because there is so much bulldozing of land and tearing down of old barns to build strip malls. One of my goals is to record nature's beauty in my quilts before it disappears.

___

DESIGN NOTEBOOK

Some of the best advice I can give on learning to design is to keep a notebook of ideas – anything that strikes you as interesting or important. Your notebooks may expand to file cabinets full of information that you collect over the years. Using a design notebook is a time-honored concept artists rely on to help them record and work out their ideas. I love going to exhibits and seeing an artist's book of notes and sketches. What a way to get a real sense of how an idea develops into a piece of art.

Starting a design notebook may give you the impetus to turn your ideas into original work. Record everything from general ideas to particular stitch combinations you want to remember. Even a quick walk in your yard can suggest an

amazing array of flower combinations and colors. Your sketches don't have to be fancy drawings and you don't have to show them to anyone. A design notebook is a great way to become more aware of your surroundings and to store your ideas until you decide what to do with them.

___

Here are some things I put in my design notebooks:
- ▸ Sketches of flowers, leaves, grasses – sometimes together in a small scene
- ▸ Block designs from interesting quilts
- ▸ Stylized motifs which might translate well into appliqué
- ▸ Sketches of buildings – for their shape or window and door placement
- ▸ Detailed sketches of stitches and their repeat patterns
- ▸ Descriptive notes of ideas for quilts
- ▸ Color combinations that appeal to me, such as the colors in a sunset, a country garden, or a meadow in winter
- ▸ Linear designs that might be adapted into quilting lines
- ▸ Names of people I meet and shops I visit
- ▸ Notes about interesting quilts at quilt shows
- ▸ Fabric samples I am looking to match or find more of
- ▸ List of favorite silk ribbon colors
- ▸ Embroidery stitches to create flowers that I see

___

I keep several spiral notebooks handy for recording ideas. I do not draw most of my appliqué work ahead of time nor do I make patterns or templates. I never could draw well and it scares me to even think about it. I have developed my own methods of cutting fabric directly into petals and flowers. However, I constantly record ideas with words or rough sketches in my notebooks. This helps me to remember them while I develop them mentally and prepare to begin a piece. I have themes I work with frequently. I store my ideas as little sketches or descriptive paragraphs. I also take lots of photographs which help me hang onto the ideas I have until I can make them up into quilts.

GETTING STARTED WITH DESIGNING

If you are following the suggestions in this chapter so far, you may have worked on your awareness of color in the natural word, pinpointed an inspiration you wish to develop into a piece of some sort, and scribbled endless ideas in your design notebook. Now, you ask, what to do next?

Designing is a process. I may turn an idea around in my head for months, thinking about how to approach it. Will it be a picture quilt? What element will be the main focus? Should I try to interpret my idea in blocks or a horizontal format? Sometimes I do a rough sketch of my idea, but more often I just note the things I want to include and work them in as I go. However, this comes after years of designing my own quilts and, certainly, was not the starting point for the designs used in my earliest work.

Creativity can be hard work, and it certainly needs inspiration, but from then on it takes planning and organization of the idea. After you have the inspiration, you need to make a start – often this is the point where we stop or hesitate due to fears we may have. If you are hesitant about trying original designs, begin with a small silk ribbon sampler. It is a way to experiment with stitches, combinations, and colors on a small

scale which may be less intimidating than jumping right in on a large quilt. Try building a strand (see Chapter 6) in colors you like on a background of your choosing and then finishing it off with silk thread stitches that you have selected. This is what designing is all about – making your own choices to express an idea or to create your own interpretation of the beauty of nature.

You can make almost any design with the versatile silk ribbon, but it is especially well suited for flower designs. Flowers made with silk ribbon look very real. I make two types of flowers. One type is representational of real flowers, often using shading and the actual flower colors. The second type I call "fantasy flowers." I use them to fill in an area or to create interest. They are totally made up, but they look so real that people are always asking me, "What flower is this?"

Next try adding some silk ribbon to an unfinished quilt. With the added element of silk ribbon, you may come up with some new ways to finish something that has stumped you. Then take another step and expand your design ideas to encompass larger quilts, including silk ribbon, as a part of the plan from the conception of the piece. Decide whether to work in appliqué or pieced work and where you will use the silk ribbon embellishment. Choose background, primary, and accent fabrics; then take that next step and just begin.

FINDING YOUR OWN DESIGN STYLE

People design in many different ways. You need to discover how you feel most comfortable working. If have never done your own designs, you are not alone. If you have worked from patterns, I would venture to say that you have changed certain elements from time to time to personalize the quilts you are making. That is a good start. Now try to think about how you work best. If you are comfortable with patterns, then maybe you will want to sketch out your ideas and work out a formal color plan first. Many quilters feel most comfortable with some sort of written guide to follow.

Good! You can write that guide for yourself. This is a great way to design. You don't have to be an artist who can draw to do this. You do need to develop a clear idea of what you want to include on your quilt. People always are saying to me, "I can't do that." But they usually can if they know what they want to design and then take it one step further and just make a start.

I now love to design as I go, letting each thing I do suggest the color or shape for the next element. However, I have disliked working from patterns all my life, so I have developed my own style of working which eliminates patterns altogether. I go straight to cutting out fabric, which works for me since appliqué doesn't require as precise measurement as piecework.

One way to help you define your design style is to think about how you like to cook. How do you use a recipe? When I cook, I look up the dish I want to make in three or four cookbooks and then pick and choose ingredients from each of them. I rarely follow the recipe exactly, often adding other ingredients as well. Since I have been cooking a long time and know a lot of basics, things usually come out fine. I like the challenge of creating as I go both when I cook and when I quilt.

Some of my friends who are excellent cooks take the opposite approach. They use a recipe as a definite guide to follow step by step. Their ways of cooking and mine are both great ways to cook. They know how they like to cook and feel comfortable doing it that way, and I feel the same way about my cooking style. The same ideas hold true for design work.

VARIATION VERSUS REPLICATION

Being aware of a balance of variation and repetition will expand your design capabilities. Quilters have traditionally repeated and varied quilt blocks throughout the history of quiltmaking. Variations, even small changes, offset repetition which can become boring. This is one reason many pieced block quilts have appliquéd borders or fancy sashing (both good places to add a little silk ribbon). Some quilt guilds offer their members the "challenge" of creating unique quilts from the same set of fabrics. The resulting quilts show great variation in design. A repeated quilt block can be varied by changing the pieced elements, or more often by just changing the colors.

Replication or exact duplication, on the other hand, does not offer as much chance for fun or interesting design possibilities as does variation. The Japanese culture has a word, "sabi", which roughly translates as "happy accident." My quilts are full of happy accidents where I ran out of fabric or ribbon and the resulting improvisation was much more interesting than the original plan.

Another way to look at variation versus replication is to think of music. In choosing a theme and repeating it, a composer makes it familiar to the ear. Then the theme may be varied in different ways to challenge the listener, such as changing the tempo and bringing in new instruments. Now imagine if a composer wrote a theme and then merely performed it exactly the same way 20 times. Instead of being a variation, it would be a mere replication and of little interest.

In nature you find lots of repetition (think of a field of wildflowers for example), but with tremendous variation in color, shape, and size. Some variations are bold and some are subtle. While a floral design with only replicated elements would look boring and unnatural, it is good to repeat some elements to add continuity

Dried flower inspired design. Cathy Grafton.

Detail of dried flower inspired design. Cathy Grafton.

to your design. The trick is to strike an interesting but harmonious balance between repetition and variation. Varying the placement, shape, and color of silk ribbon floral designs makes the embellishment look more like nature. Exact duplication over and over becomes tedious both to the artist and the viewer.

Here are several suggestions for creating repeated but varied elements in silk ribbon embroidery. Use repeated colors in the stems and leaves but vary the flower shapes and colors. Repeat the shapes and curves of stems or strands of flowers but vary the silk ribbon and thread colors. On a larger quilt, add variation by working silk ribbon on a repeated block pattern. The basic idea is simple: keep some things the same and change others.

DRIED FLOWER DESIGNS

If you really feel uncomfortable with a "blank canvas," you may want to begin by trying the designs presented in Chapter 8 and adding some of your own ideas to them. You could also try looking at a book, picture or drawing of a flower grouping and recreating it on fabric. Using a dried flower grouping is a good transition from pre-marked designs to spontaneous placement. By working a small piece for practice, you can learn a lot about natural placement of flowers. You will gain confidence with each piece you work and I hope that in time you will feel comfortable with the freedom of unmarked or minimally marked designs.

Silk ribbon flowers and pressed flower arrangements have a similar feel. You can use a dried flower picture – the real thing or from a library book on dried flower arranging – to recreate some of those designs in silk ribbon on fabric. In dried flower arrangements, stems of leaves,

Wildflower Sampler. Cathy Grafton.

Swiss Spring. Designed and made by Cathy Grafton. 1994. Collection of Gaston
and Klara Scheidegger. Vevey, Switzerland.

Joe's Blue Heron. Cathy Grafton. Collection of Joe and Mary Jobst. Pontiac, IL.

Joe's Blue Heron detail. Cathy Grafton.
Collection of Joe and Mary Jobst. Pontiac, IL.

stalks of flowers, and seed pods are grouped to form a design pleasing in color and shape. One of my small samplers is based on a dried flower picture I saw and quickly sketched to help me recreate the placement. What fun to choose the silk ribbon stitches I thought best matched the flowers and leaves I had seen in that picture.

Embellishing with a floral spray

MARKING YOUR DESIGNS

Before you transfer a design onto your background, determine if it is really necessary to mark the placement of each stitch and flower. Very often you will find that if you mark a few general guidelines to help you envision your design, your imagination will be free to embellish the work as you go. For instance, if you are embellishing with a floral spray which will be gathered by a couched ribbon bow, consider lightly marking just a few flower placements, such as a "Y" shape for a spider web rose, and a few pencil lines to show the lines the flowers will follow. See illustration at left.

From there, let your imagination work as you fill in the other areas with flowers and combination stitches until you feel the colors and shapes reach a pleasing balance.

ADDING SILK RIBBON TO YOUR QUILTS

You may be like me – someone whose best expression of an idea is through appliqué. I dearly love it and have done it for 20 years. For me, it is the way I work best. On the other hand, you may be someone who will piece forever and dreads the thought of appliqué. Maybe you fall somewhere in between, and maybe you work exclusively by hand or by machine. Any of these quiltmaking styles can benefit from the addition of silk ribbon embellishment.

Silk ribbon on quilts can play a leading role, but more often you will use it as an accent or addition to your main design. Following are some specific ideas to help you combine silk ribbon embellishment with your own appliqué or piecework. In the next chapter, you will learn specific stitches which you can use to create the effects you want on your quilts.

SILK RIBBON AND APPLIQUÉ

I am currently using silk ribbon to embellish most of my appliqué pieces. I love how the silk ribbon and thread add texture, details, and touches of color which can highlight or echo the colors of the appliqué pieces. In addition to embellishment, silk ribbon is large enough to be combined directly with appliqué, for example, as a stem for an appliqué flower. It is also a great way to fill small empty spaces.

One reason to add silk ribbon is to help create images and moods in a quilt. For example, I often try to create the feeling of dappled sunlight. I love the feeling of shadows and sunlight combining at the edge of the deep woods with the sun shining through the leaves. To help me get this effect on a quilt, I choose fabrics carefully. Strip piecing used to be the best way to get this feeling in a quilt, but today there are many mottled fabrics which work well to give this effect. Next I add variegated silk ribbon and thread to enhance the impression of dappled light.

SILK RIBBON AND PIECEWORK

Silk ribbon is best known to quilters as an element used in crazy quilting, which reached the peak of its popularity around the turn of the century. Seam lines were covered with all sorts of embroidery and embellishment, including silk ribbon, and the blocks often had elaborate flowers, birds, baskets, dates, and initials embroidered in the centers. Crazy quilting is still a wonderful way to use silk ribbon. Because it is larger in scale than embroidery thread, silk ribbon becomes a stronger part of the design rather than a minor accent.

Since my main area of work is appliqué, my experimentation with pieced work and silk ribbon embellishment has been limited. I don't see as many ways for combining silk ribbon and piecework as I do with appliqué, but I hope that some of you will explore your own possibilities. Silk ribbon embellishment could accentuate seam lines to emphasize secondary patterns between the blocks. It could also be used to soften straight angles and lines, add a feeling of movement, and emphasize shapes in the patchwork. Quilts with machine embroidery would be a good source of inspiration for ideas beyond crazy quilts. For example, Caryl Bryer Fallert in her Aurora Borealis series used glitzy machine embroidery threads to enhance pieced lines with a dramatic effect.

Silk ribbon embellishment does not always have to be naturalistic or floral in design. If done in a stylized manner, it can lend an art deco air or linear emphasis to the design. Try stitches such as the angular triple feather stitch or accentuate a line of alternate feather stitches with several same color French knots extending off each hook to create this effect.

Jacket embellishment. Maureen Carlson.

Denim shirt embellishment. Maureen Carlson.

Shirt detail. Maureen Carlson.

Shirt detail. Maureen Carlson.

SILK RIBBON ON CLOTHING

Silk ribbon is a natural choice for embellishment of clothing. On clothing, some of the best areas for design are the front, back, sleeve, and shoulder areas or along the hem of a dress or skirt. Even a touch of ribbon on any of these areas gives a garment a distinctive and unique look. Ribbon can also add color which will enliven clothing. You can create a larger design in one place and then add variations in another area, for example, putting a basket of flowers on the back of a vest and repeating the design of several of the flowers on the collar or shoulder area. You can put silk ribbon on pieced, appliquéd, or ready-made items. Add some to vests, blouses, dresses, aprons, sweaters, or accessories.

There are a few special considerations when using silk ribbon on clothing. First of all, since clothing will be laundered more frequently, the best stitches to use are those that work up fairly tightly. Very loose stitches can fray or catch when washed. Use a little extra care when making the stitches. For instance, when making a spider web rose on clothing, take small tacking stitches in matching thread around the outer edge of the

rose to help hold it in place and prevent fraying in the wash. I would also work the rose fairly tightly to begin with, if I knew it would be washed frequently. I would not use a couched stitch unless I tacked it down with fine threads as a precaution. Very loose looped stitches are also not a good choice. However, the twisted stitches worked on a fairly small scale would work nicely. After you have some experience in working the stitches, you will be able to choose those that work best for clothing.

Placement is an important consideration also. I would not put a silk ribbon design where my purse strap rests or over a pocket where I might brush against the stitches. Being aware of how the garment is to be used and putting your silk ribbon designs in a somewhat protected area will make a big difference in how your garment will wear. Of course, you want to plan the placement to be sure your stitching will be seen.

The examples, stitched by friends and shown on these pages, show some of the variety of clothing, both handmade and ready-made, which can be graced by the addition of silk ribbon embellishment.

Designs for planning silk ribbon placement on clothing

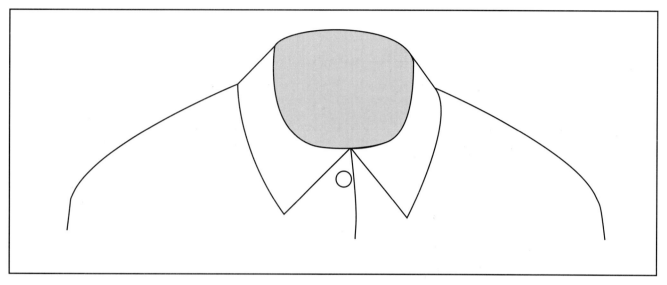

The collar area of any shirt can be used for embellishment.

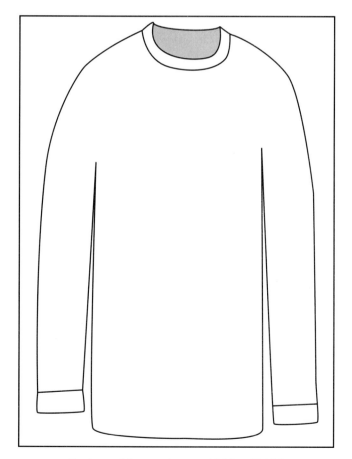

Can be used for sweater, sweatshirt, or T-shirt.

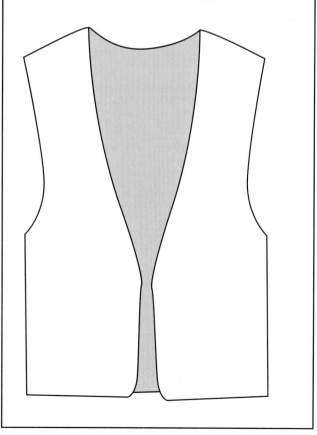

Silk ribbon designs are a good choice for vests.

Sweater with silk ribbon flowers. Lillian Cagle.

Sweater with bouquet of silk ribbon flowers placed in a woven basket made of chenille thread. Lillian Cagle.

Denim blouse with silk ribbon embellishment and appliquéd bird. Peggy Hessling.

Vest with silk ribbon flowers. Audrey Sanner. Pattern by The Granny May Company.

Denim jumper with silk ribbon embellishment. Peggy Hessling

Chapter 5

THE STITCHES

"Of female arts in usefulness
The needle far exceeds the rest
In ornament there's no device
Affords adorning half so nice."

From a sampler dated 1820, by Mary Ann Morton, Portland, Maine

INTRODUCTION

Embroidery is a traditional style of decorative art in almost every world culture. Countries, ethnic groups, and even eras all have distinctive stitches and designs. Certain styles and stitches have been a part of sewing history since the first cave women used a bone needle and sinew to fashion crude garments. Decoration of garments and later household goods was not far behind. To me, the use of decorative stitching on fabric is a basic expression of the need we all have to bring beauty into our everyday lives.

The stitches used for silk ribbon embellishment are for the most part simple, basic stitches. With few exceptions, these stitches have been used for centuries by women and men to decorate clothing, linens, and quilts, and have been passed from generation to generation. If you are an embroiderer, then you know most of them already. If you have never done embroidery, you will find they become easier to stitch with just a little practice. Keep this in mind and perhaps plan a practice piece to experiment on until you get comfortable working the stitches.

The stitches shown here are only several of the hundreds of stitches and variations known to embroiderers. I show you only a few for several reasons. I have found that much of the variety created with silk ribbon comes from color changes and stitch combinations. I find I tend to use a few favorite stitches over and over, changing their colors and the way I combine them. Your choices may be different from mine, so once you get comfortable with using the ribbon to embroider, you can experiment with some of the other stitches to find your own special favorites.

It is important to have a good descriptive guide of the basic stitches to help you learn first how to make them and then how best to use them. There are literally hundreds of books on embroidery which list stitches and endless variations on those stitches, and these books are great resources. (See Bibliography at the end of this book.)

I have found that those new to embroidery can find manipulation of silk ribbon difficult and frustrating at first. In this chapter I give a written description of how to make each stitch along with illustrations. If you are experienced in working these stitches in cotton embroidery floss, you will find them almost the same to make with ribbon. Most of these stitches can be worked with either silk ribbon or silk thread – each with a different effect – and I have noted where they work best with either one or the other.

It is often easier to work a stitch from left to right or vice versa, and I note when this should be done. (If you are left-handed, you will need to reverse many of these descriptions when you form the stitches.) In some cases you will also want to work top to bottom or bottom to top to minimize wasting ribbon on the back of the piece. I also note this where applicable, but depending on how you use the stitches in your own work, this may change. It is best if you teach yourself to be aware of where to begin a line of stitching in order to minimize wasting ribbon on the back side of your work.

Stitch size varies from person to person as in knitting and other needlework. Different people tend to work their stitches larger or smaller. As you work with silk ribbon embroidery, you will discover what works best for you.

I have selected stitches from four families of traditional stitches and have also added a section on combination stitches which include some special flowers, grasses, couched bows, fans, and medallions. Directions are given using 4 mm ribbon, but please feel free to experiment with 7 mm or 2 mm if you wish.

See Chapter 3 for tips on working with silk ribbon, including controlling fraying and twisting of the ribbon and instructions on beginning, knotting, and ending a silk ribbon.

Stitch Glossary

Flat stitches
stem stitch
outline stitch
straight stitch
ribbon stitch (ribbon only)
cross-stitch

Loop stitches
alternating feather stitch
single feather stitch
triple feather stitch
fly stitch
extended fly stitch
plume stitch (ribbon)
twisted plume stitch (ribbon)

Knots
French knot
colonial knot
coral stitch
pistil stitch

Chain stitches
chain stitch
whipped chain stitch
detached chain stitch (lazy daisy)
filled lazy daisy stitch
detached twisted chain stitch
split stitch (thread only)

Combination stitches
spider web rose
buds (rose and other)
leaves and the calyx
grapes, berries, and clumps
feather stitch ferns
baby's breath filler
cone flowers
dandelions and fly stitch flowers
snowdrops and hanging flowers
grasses and sedges
feathers, fur, and hair
facial features
ruffles and flourishes – couched bows
and ribbons
fans and medallions
spider webs and spiders

Flat Stitches

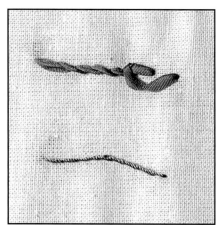

Stem Stitch
(Ribbon and Thread)

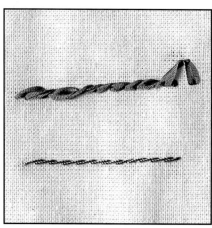

Outline Stitch
(Ribbon and Thread)

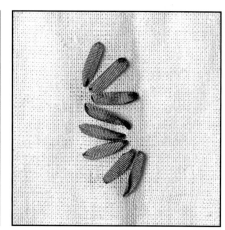

Straight Stitch

The first stitches illustrated here are flat stitches. These simple stitches are the basis for many flowers and leaves. They make good filler stitches and most of them may be worked using either ribbon or embroidery thread.

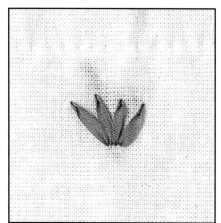

Ribbon Stitch

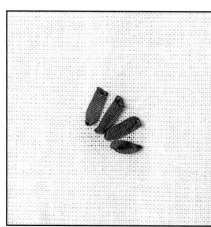

Ribbon Stitch Variation

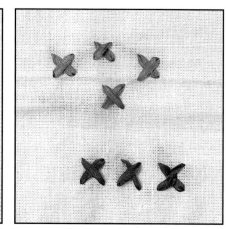

Cross Stitch and Cross Stitch Variation

STEM STITCH
(or crewel outline stitch)

The stem stitch, as the name implies, is used to make stems. It is sometimes confused with the outline stitch. They are made in a slightly different way and have different effects. The stem stitch gives a blended line. The difference may not be apparent when you use ribbon, but is more so with thread. This stitch is useful for making stems and defining lines.

WORK left to right coming up at A and going down at B, then coming up at C halfway between A and B. Keep the ribbon *below* your stitch line as you pull the ribbon through. Now go down at D and come back up at B, pulling the ribbon through. Continue in this manner until you have the length stem you wish. This stitch may be worked with ribbon or thread.

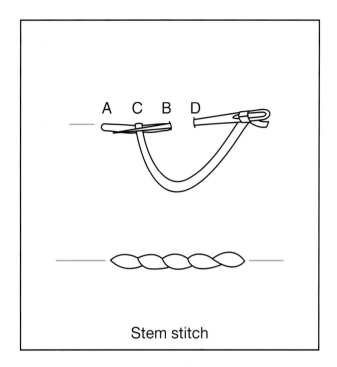

Stem stitch

OUTLINE STITCH

The outline stitch is also used to make stems, but gives a slightly textured and usually more definite line. When worked in thread, this stitch looks continuous so that you are not aware of where each stitch begins.

WORK left to right coming up at A and going down at B, keeping the ribbon *above* your needle and stitch line. As in the stem stitch, come back half way with the needle and come out at C. Continue the stitch, keeping the ribbon above your needle as you work. If stitching around curves, take very tiny stitches to keep a smooth line.

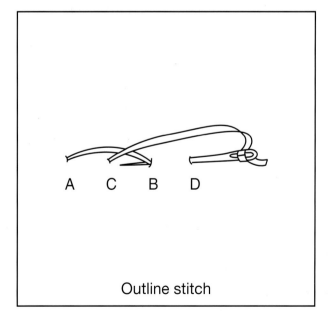

Outline stitch

Straight stitch

STRAIGHT STITCH
(or stab stitch)

This stitch is useful for making petals, ferns, and leaves. Some care must be taken to keep the ribbon flat without twisting for the best effect. It should not be pulled too tightly, but kept slightly loose. This is a good stitch for using variegated ribbon.

WORK the straight stitch by coming up at A and going down at B, varying the length of this stitch depending on the effect you desire. You will need to practice to keep the ribbon from twisting as you go down into B; using short lengths of ribbon will help here. It is best to hold the ribbon flat with your left hand or use a trolley needle (see page 27) to keep it from twisting as you pull it through.

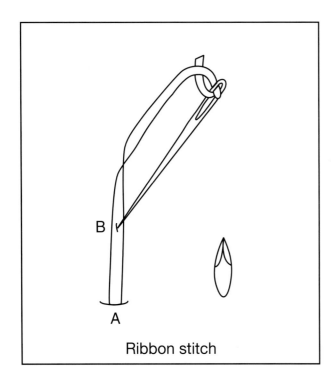

Ribbon stitch

RIBBON STITCH
(or inverted stab stitch,
Japanese ribbon stitch)

This versatile stitch is one worked only with ribbon. I have seen it on old crazy quilts from the turn of the century so it has been around for some time. It is one of the most beautiful stitches to use in ribbon work yet is quite simple to make. It is especially good for petals or leaves.

WORK by coming up at A, holding the ribbon flat on the background with your left hand. Then pierce the ribbon with the needle as you go down into the back at B. Holding your left thumb on the ribbon as you pull the needle through the fabric helps stabilize the ribbon. This stitch must not be pulled too tightly or you will have a straight line of ribbon. As you pull the needle, toward the back, the ribbon will bunch up, and as it pulls through to the tip of the ribbon, it will curl slightly. A variation of this stitch is to leave the bunched up ribbon as a small topknot instead of pulling it through. This is especially good for a fern effect.

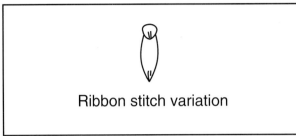

Ribbon stitch variation

CROSS-STITCH

This stitch is very old and widely used in decorative embroidery. It is a classic stitch used by women to mark linens and has had many variations and revivals. In silk ribbon work it is good for making small flowers or for background filler.

WORK this stitch by coming out at A to make a slanted stitch and going in at B, and then coming out at C. Cross your first stitch, going down again at D. You may continue in a line of stitching, scatter them in the background, or add a small horizontal stitch at the cross of the stitches to make a flower. The small stitch may be done with a contrasting color, if desired.

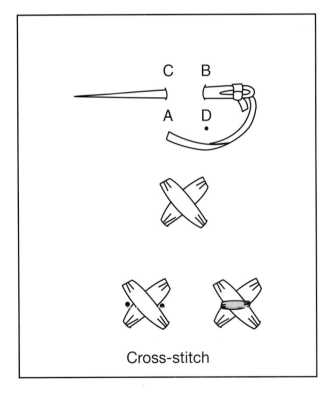

Cross-stitch

Loop Stitches

Alternating Feather
(Ribbon and Thread)

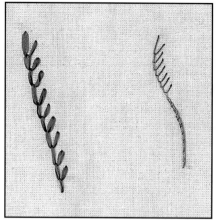

Single Feather
(Ribbon and Thread)

Triple Feather
(Ribbon and Thread)

Loop stitches are a large family of stitches which are usually curved in some manner and then tied down with a smaller catch stitch. The many variations can usually be worked with either ribbon or thread. The feather stitch especially looks entirely different when worked with ribbon, and forms an excellent base on which to stitch many flowers.

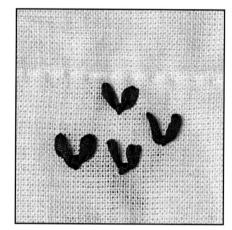

Fly Stitch

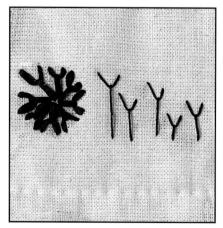

Extended Fly Stitch
(Ribbon and Thread)

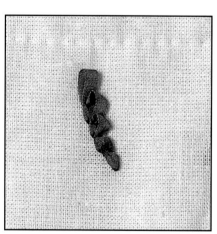

Plume Stitch
(Ribbon)

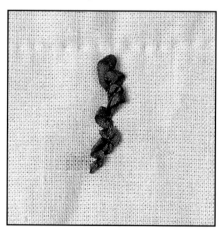

Twisted Plume Stitch
(Ribbon)

ALTERNATING FEATHER STITCH

There are two primary ways to work a feather stitch, each with countless variations. You will find this stitch very versatile for use with both ribbon and thread. This stitch is great for flower stems, ferns, grasses, and bunches of flowers. It is also a good stitch for decorative border designs. The angle at which you put the needle in will give different effects. Experiment with this stitch!

WORK this stitch from top to bottom of your piece to minimize wasted ribbon on the back. Come out at A and go down to the right at B, leaving a loop of ribbon *below* your work. Come out below A at C (at this point your needle should angle as if going from 2 to 7 on the face of a clock) and pull the ribbon snugly up, catching the loop to hold it down. Then turn your needle to go in to the right of C at D, coming out below A at E (the needle now should angle as if going from 10 to 5 on the face of a clock), again catching the loop as you snug up the ribbon. Continue on downward, alternating the angle of the needle with each stitch. This is an easy stitch once you understand it. Check the diagram as you go.

SINGLE FEATHER STITCH

You will find that working the feather stitch in one direction will seem easier than the other. Work the single feather stitch going in the direction easier for you for practice.

WORK the single feather stitch from top to bottom of your piece, coming out at A and going in at B, keeping the loop of ribbon *below and on the same side* as you make the stitch. Come out below A at C and continue going in at D and coming out at E. You should be able to get a rhythm going which makes this a pleasant stitch to work.

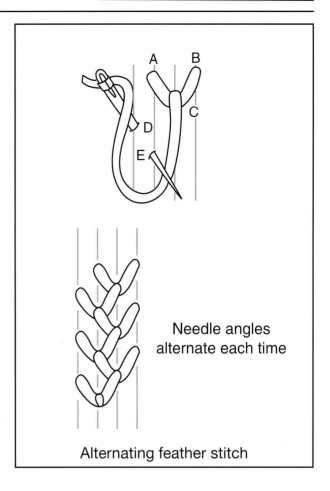

Needle angles alternate each time

Alternating feather stitch

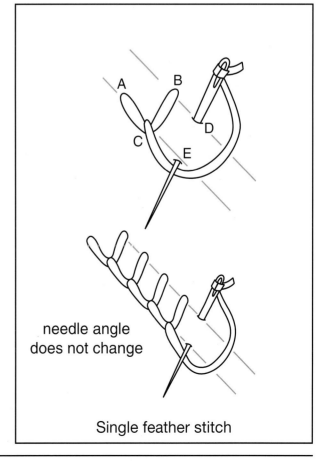

needle angle does not change

Single feather stitch

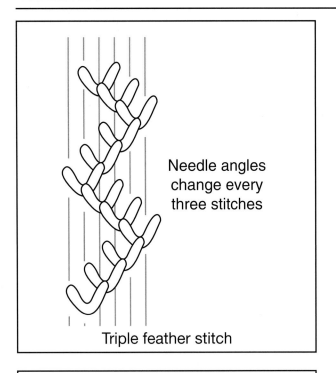

Needle angles change every three stitches

Triple feather stitch

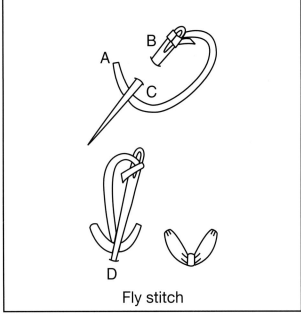

Fly stitch

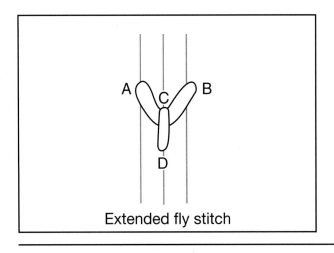

Extended fly stitch

TRIPLE FEATHER STITCH

Again, there are numerous variations to this stitch and it is often combined with other stitches, as will be shown in the combination section. Here is one variation, the triple feather stitch, which is quite nice to use on art deco or other stylized work.

WORK this stitch by making three feather stitches to the right and then three to the left, moving downward as you go. The angle of inserting the needle and different stitch lengths affect how it looks. When you master this stitch, use your imagination. It is effective whether done with ribbon or thread.

FLY STITCH

This is a neat little stitch which can be effective alone as a single flower or layered and grouped in different ways. It can be worked with ribbon or thread.

WORK from left to right coming out at A and going in at B, keeping the loop of ribbon *below* your needle. Come out at C and secure the loop by going down at D.

EXTENDED FLY STITCH

This interesting variation, very effective with silk threads, is good for working petals, weeds or in circles for flowers.

WORK from left to right, coming out at A and going in at B, keeping the loop of ribbon or thread *below* your needle. Come out at C with your needle and go down at D to secure the loop and make a stem.

PLUME STITCH
(or loop stitch)

This stitch can be worked singly or in rows. A trolley needle (see Chapter 3) may help you make this stitch. Keeping the ribbon from twisting may be difficult at first. If you have a lot of trouble, try the twisted plume stitch.

WORK by coming up with the needle at A and going down at B, leaving a small loop. Hold the loop with the trolley needle or a toothpick while you come up through the ribbon at C to secure the stitch. Do not snug up the loop. Go down again at D, holding the next loop until you come up through the ribbon at E to secure that stitch. Continue until you wish to end the plume which can be done with a small stitch to the back or a French knot. To make a single loop, go in at B as in the plume, come out at C, and make a small stitch or French knot to secure the loop.

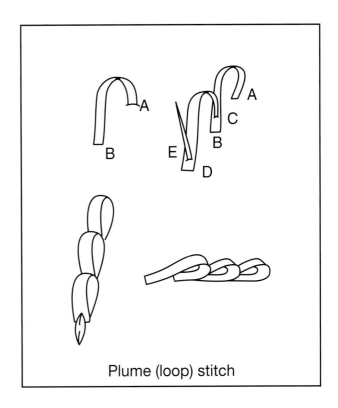

Plume (loop) stitch

TWISTED PLUME

This stitch gives a free-form look to flower petals. You may find you enjoy making this stitch more than the regular plume.

WORK the twisted plume by coming up at A and going down at B. However, let the ribbon twist as you leave your loop. Come up at C, holding the loop with a trolley needle until secured. Continue until you wish to end by making a small stitch to the back or a French knot.

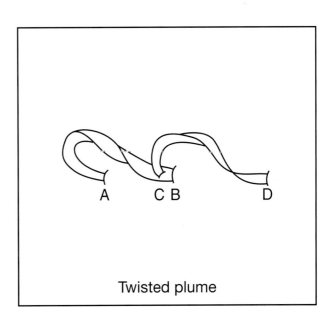

Twisted plume

Knots

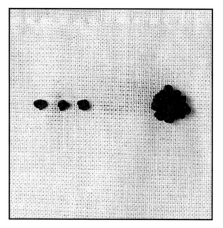
French Knot

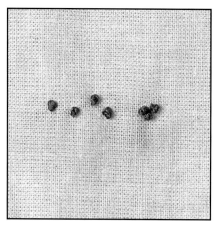
Colonial Knot

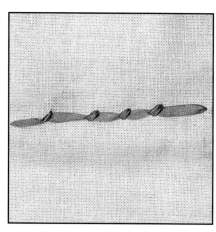
Coral Stitch
(Ribbon)

Knot stitches add wonderful texture to your work and look especially interesting when done with ribbon. The French knot is either loved or hated by most embroiderers. I show the colonial knot as an alternative to the French knot if you have problems making the French knot. However, I see little difference between them when made with ribbon.

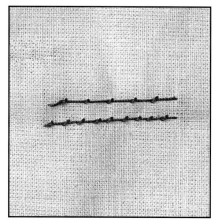
Coral Stitch
(Thread)

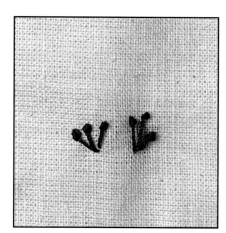
Pistil Stitch
(Thread)

FRENCH KNOT

French knots can be done as a single detached stitch or in rows or lines. Usually with ribbon it is done as a detached single stitch. It is a most effective stitch for embellishing and is included in several of the combination stitches shown later in this chapter. French knots are often clustered, and when worked this way are very effective done in shaded ribbons.

WORK the French knot by bringing the needle up from the back and wrapping the ribbon around it twice near the point. Holding the ribbon with your left hand, insert the point of the needle near but not in the same hole you came out of. Continue to hold the ribbon snug on the needle with your left hand as you pull it through to the back.

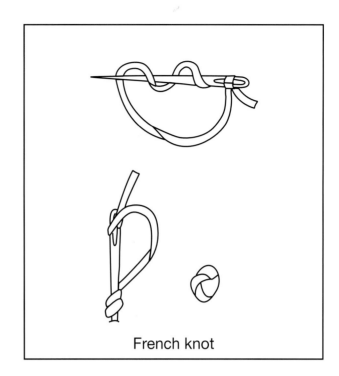

French knot

COLONIAL KNOT

I must admit that I never could figure out how to do a colonial knot until someone demonstrated it for me. I find it a little harder to work than a French knot, but some stitchers prefer it. Try them both and decide which one you like best.

WORK the colonial knot by coming up from the back. Point the needle back toward the fabric and hold the ribbon with your left hand. Maneuver the needle first over, then under a loop of ribbon near where it came out. Then with your left hand, bring the ribbon over the needle to form a loose figure eight. Insert the point of the needle into the background near but not in the same hole. With your left hand, keep the ribbon snug to the needle as you pull it through.

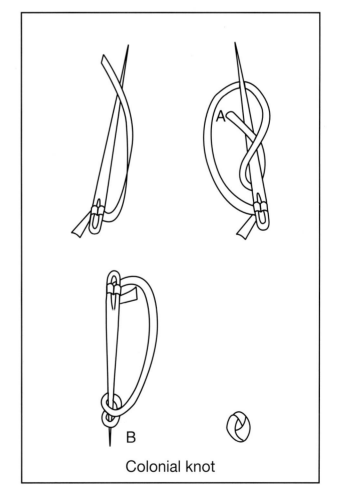

Colonial knot

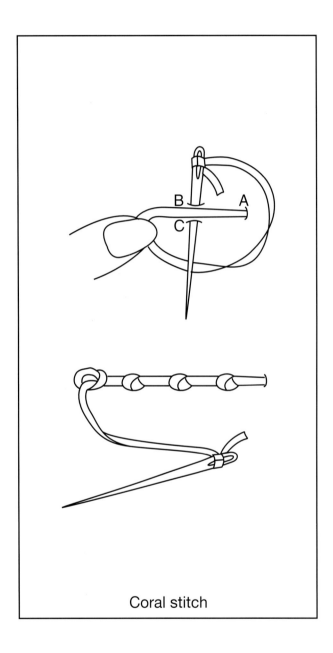

Coral stitch

CORAL STITCH

This stitch gives you a textured line of knots and may be used with thread or ribbon. It can be used as a decorative filler and for bunches of grass or stems. The knots can be spaced closely together to give an almost beaded effect.

WORK the coral stitch from right to left, coming out at A and then holding your ribbon down with your left thumb in the direction you wish to go. Now going in at B just above the ribbon, take a small slanted stitch, coming out at C. It is important that you catch the loop of ribbon to make this knot.

PISTIL STITCH

I love this little stitch. It is nothing more than a French knot at the end of a stitch. It is, as the name suggests, useful in creating flower pistils and can add touches of color anywhere you desire. It adds complexity to flowers, whether grouped or used singly. While it may also be done with ribbon, I think you will find this stitch most effective when done with silk thread.

WORK a pistil stitch coming up from the back at A, making a French knot by wrapping the thread twice around the point of the needle, and then going down at B. Be sure to hold the length of thread snugly with your left hand as you pull the thread through to be sure your knot does not come undone. Secure on the back or continue with another pistil stitch.

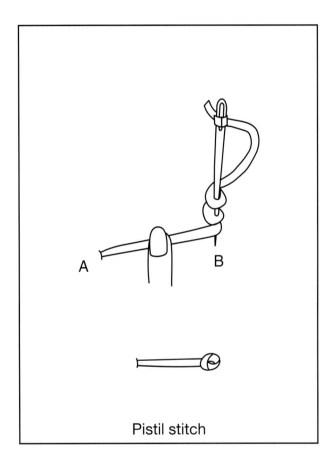

Pistil stitch

Chain Stitches

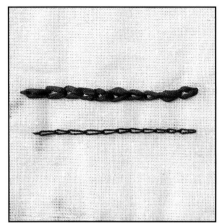

Chain Stitch
(Ribbon and Thread)

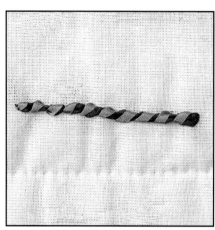

Whipped Chain Stitch

Detached Chain Stitch
(Lazy Daisy)

The chain stitches include some old friends like the lazy daisy, which is familiar to anyone who did embroidery as a child. I am showing three with a few variations to get you started. Chain stitches are closed loop stitches done either as a connected chain or in a detached form. They make wonderful petals, leaves, and stems. Chain stitches are quite decorative as borders and for stylized work.

Filled Lazy Daisy

Detached Twisted Chain Stitch

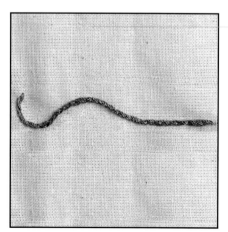

Split Stitch
(Thread)

CHAIN STITCH

The basic chain stitch is a connected loop of stitches with very little waste of ribbon on the back. It works quite well for stems, especially if you use the whipped variation in a contrasting ribbon. It may be worked in ribbon or thread.

WORK the chain stitch either top to bottom or right to left. Start by coming out at A and making a loop with the ribbon. Hold the loop down loosely with your left hand and insert the needle again at A, making a stitch coming out at B. Snug up the loop as you pull the ribbon through and continue with another loop held down by the left hand, inserting the needle this time at B and making a stitch coming out at C. To end, hold down the last loop with a small stitch into the background.

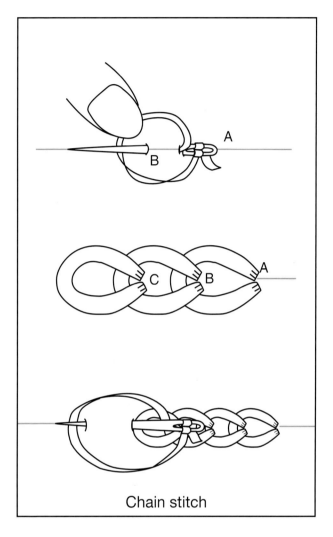

Chain stitch

WHIPPED CHAIN STITCH

Make a line of chain stitching as described above and add a second ribbon or thread to "whip" around each stitch by passing under and over the chain stitches without stitching into any background material. Do not go into the background until you finish off.

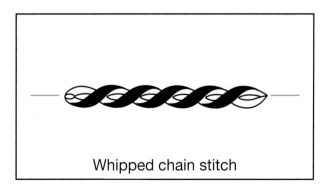

Whipped chain stitch

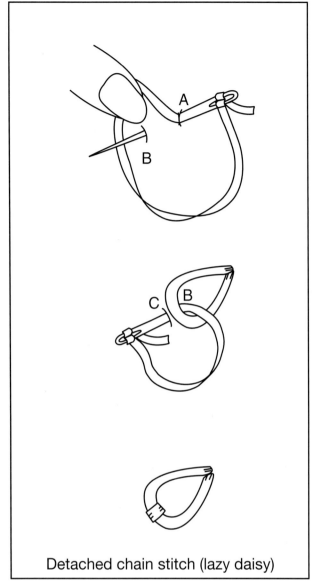

Detached chain stitch (lazy daisy)

DETACHED CHAIN STITCH
(or lazy daisy)

The beloved lazy daisy stitch was one of the first taught when I was young. It is easy to make and always effective. It is simply a single version of the chain stitch which may be placed in circle formations to make flowers. When done in green, this stitch makes wonderful leaves.

WORK a lazy daisy by coming up at A and looping the ribbon ahead of the needle, holding it flat with your left thumb. Insert the point of the needle at A again and take a stitch on the back coming out at B with the ribbon looped under your needle. Snug up the loop and secure it with a small catch stitch at C.

FILLED LAZY DAISY

You can add a second color to a lazy daisy petal with a small straight stitch worked inside the loop. After making a lazy daisy stitch, take a second color and come up at A, make a small straight stitch and come down inside the loop near the catch stitch.

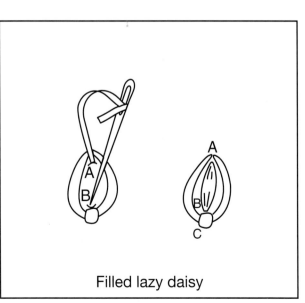

Filled lazy daisy

DETACHED TWISTED CHAIN STITCH

I find this to be one of the most versatile and interesting stitches for use with silk ribbon. It can be used for leaves, flowers, petals, and as a filler. It is a little bit tricky, but once you understand how it works, I think you will enjoy making it. The beauty of the stitch is that each one comes out a little bit differently – just as petals and leaves do in nature. This stitch is more closed than the lazy daisy.

WORK this stitch similar to the lazy daisy stitch. If you use it to add random petals, work it from bottom to top to minimize wasted ribbon on the back. Come out at A and loop the ribbon to the right ahead of the needle, holding it down with your left thumb and letting the ribbon twist. Now, instead of going back into the same hole, go to the right of A at B, taking a stitch in the back and coming up inside the loop at C. Hold down the loop by making a small catch stitch, stitching into the background at D. As an alternative, you may make the loop to the left, hold it down and then go to the left of A before going in. It doesn't matter how you form the stitch as long as you get the ribbon to twist as the stitch is formed.

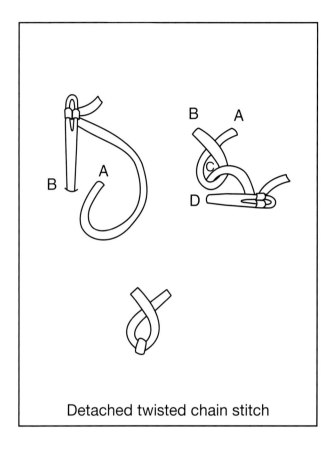

Detached twisted chain stitch

SPLIT STITCH

This is a good filler stitch for use with thread only. It can also be used for outlining and lettering. You will want to use an untwisted or loosely twisted thread for this stitch for the best effect. Use a thread that is four-ply or more for this stitch.

WORK left to right coming out at A and going down at B, then coming up at C and splitting the thread. Continue going down at D and coming back up at B, again splitting the thread.

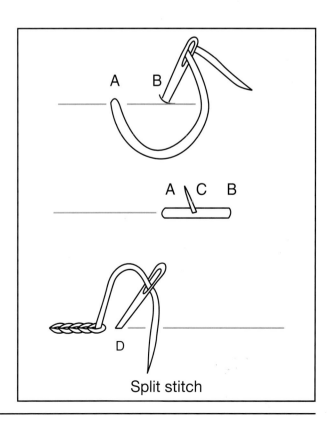

Split stitch

Combination Stitches

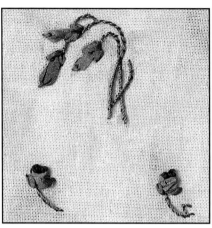

Spider Web Rose   **Buds (Rose and Other)**   **Leaves** (Detached Twisted Chain, Straight Stitch)

As you practice the stitches in this book, you will start to come up with your own ideas for combinations to make special flowers and other design elements. This section will help you get started by giving you some examples of combinations that I have found useful in my own work. You will soon have your own favorite stitches, and when you say to yourself, "I wonder what would happen if I tried this stitch and added that stitch?", you will know it is time to follow that thought and do some experimenting to create your own combinations.

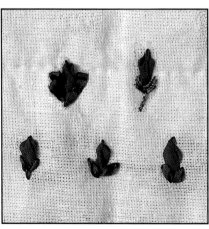

Leaves
(Lazy Daisy, Ribbon Stitch)

Calyx (Fly, Ribbon, Straight, Plume, and Fly in Thread)

Clumps, Grapes, and Berries

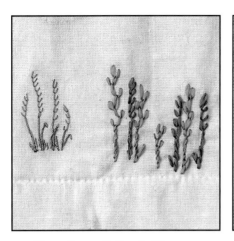

Feather Stitch Ferns
(Thread and Ribbon)

Feather Stitch Ferns Variation
(Thread and Ribbon)

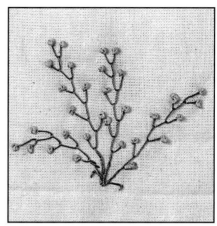

Baby's Breath Filler

Coneflowers

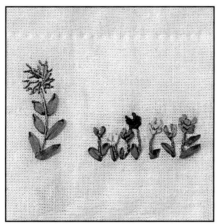

Fly Stitch Flowers

Snowdrop Flower

Hanging Flowers

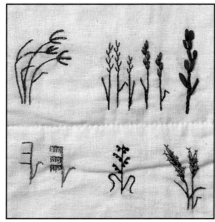

Grasses

Fly Stitch Birds and Bird
(Silk Ribbon Details)

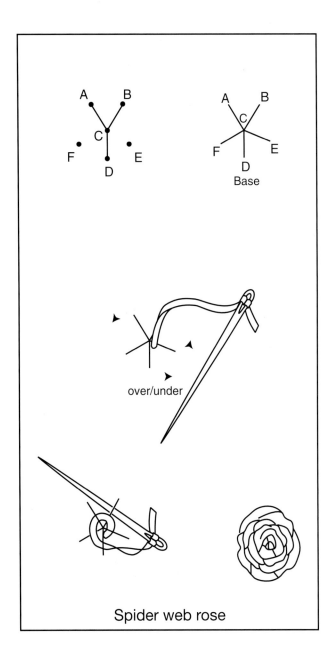

Base

over/under

Spider web rose

SPIDER WEB ROSE

There are many forms of ribbon roses. I love the easy spider web rose and think it one of the most realistic looking. It is worked on a thread base. The ribbon is woven onto the base to create the rose. You may wish to use a blunt tapestry needle to weave the ribbon. In this stitch let your ribbon twist to make the rose look more realistic. Use similar colors for the thread base and ribbon.

WORK a thread base (I like to use quilting thread for strength) starting with a fly stitch which forms a "Y" shape. Come out at A and loop the thread *below* the needle, going in at B and coming out at C to catch the loop. Go into the background at D, trying to keep the "spokes" of the "Y" equal. Now make two more spokes, coming up at point E, and go into the background in the center at C, coming up at F, and then into the background again at C. You now have a thread wheel of five roughly equal spokes. Now with your ribbon, come up from the back near the center of your wheel. Weave the ribbon over and under the spokes, weaving round and round in a spiral, letting it twist and turn as you go. Do not stitch into the background fabric, but weave the ribbon over and under the thread base. Continue until you can no longer see the spokes or have reached the size rose you desire. Then go through to the back and tie off your ribbon.

If any of your spoke ends still show, cover them with leaves or other embellishment of the rose. A larger rose can be the focal point of your design, or you can scatter smaller roses on a strand. A variation would be to begin with a French knot center using a contrasting ribbon color. This is best done after making the thread base but before weaving the ribbon, which minimizes the risk of pulling your rose out of shape.

BUDS (rose and other)

Buds are a small detail which can add lots of appeal to your work. If you are adding a bud to another flower, you will want to repeat the color of the flower. Buds can also be grouped or scattered in a background.

There are lots of ways to work a bud. I have illustrated just a few. Most buds require at least two colors of silk ribbon to look realistic. When doing buds, consider adding a calyx (the leafy part of the flower) to make it look more real.

WORK a small rose bud by starting with two French knots next to each other in your first color. With the second ribbon color, begin along the left side of the knots. Come up at A and do a straight stitch that goes down at B below the second (right) French knot. Now come up at C to the right of the knots and do another straight stitch, going down at D below the first (left) French knot. This means your stitches will crisscross in a herringbone pattern. For a very small bud, stop there, or repeat with two more straight stitches for a larger bud. Add a calyx (see the section on leaves and the calyx, page 73) with green ribbon or silk thread and attach the bud to the other flowers with a stem stitch done in silk thread.

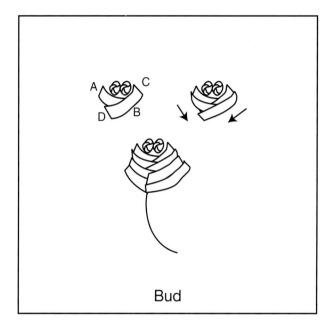

Bud

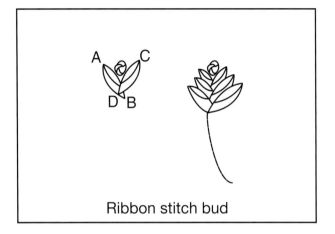

Ribbon stitch bud

RIBBON STITCH BUD VARIATION

A delicate bud can be made with one or two French knots in the center surrounded by several ribbon stitches.

WORK this bud by starting with a ribbon French knot. In a second color make a ribbon stitch from the left of the knot at A to below the knot at B. Now make a second ribbon stitch from the right side of the knot at C to below the first stitch at D. Continue until you have the size bud you wish. Add a green ribbon calyx with two small straight stitches or with silk thread with the fly stitch. Attach the buds to the flowers with green silk thread stem stitch.

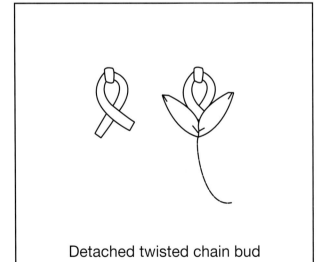

Detached twisted chain bud

DETACHED TWISTED CHAIN BUD VARIATION

A detached twisted chain stitch also makes a good bud. These can be grouped on stems or in a bunch.

WORK by doing a single detached twisted chain stitch for each bud. Then with green silk ribbon, make a small straight stitch on each side of the base of the bud to form the calyx. Attach the buds with green silk thread stems or group them close together for a bouquet effect.

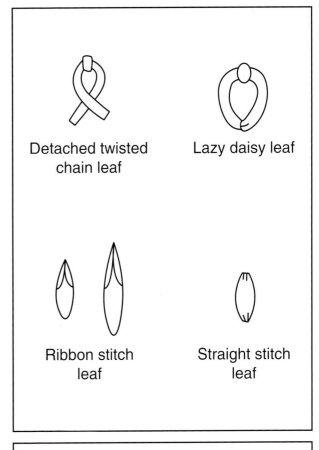

Detached twisted chain leaf

Lazy daisy leaf

Ribbon stitch leaf

Straight stitch leaf

LEAVES AND THE CALYX

Leaves add realism to your floral work, and also fill in spaces, blend colors, and provide color accents. I suggest using three to five greens if you are making lots of leaves. There are many different colors of green in nature. Leaves can be made with many of the same stitches you use for flowers – detached twisted chain, lazy daisy, ribbon stitch, and straight stitch. Explore ways to make leaves and add them freely to your work.

The calyx is the small leafy part under a flower. A calyx adds a finished look to your flowers. They can be worked with thread or ribbon and usually should match the stem color. Try a fly stitch, ribbon stitch, straight stitch, or plume stitch to form them. If you want a heavier look, work them in ribbon. For just a touch of green or a lighter shape, use thread.

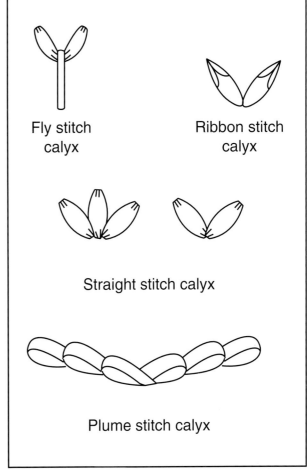

Fly stitch calyx

Ribbon stitch calyx

Straight stitch calyx

Plume stitch calyx

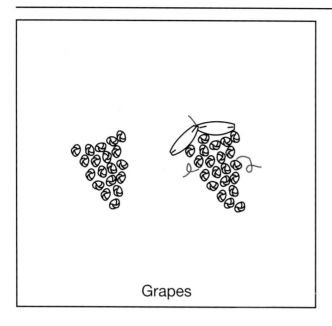

Grapes

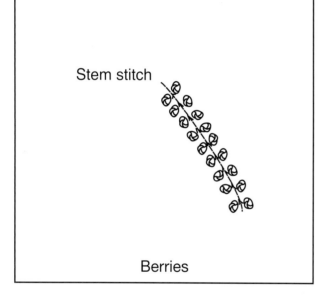

Stem stitch

Berries

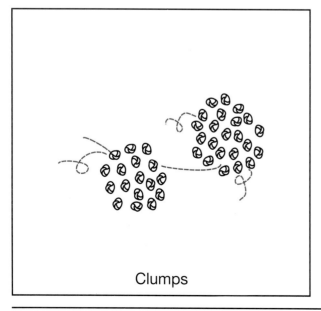

Clumps

GRAPES, BERRIES, AND CLUMPS

You can use the versatile French knot to make all sorts of grapes, seeds, berries, and miscellaneous clumps. To shade grapes, use three colors of ribbon or a variegated ribbon. Your color choices and the shape of your clumps will define whether your clumps are grapes, berries or seeds or just a fantasy clump of some sort. Clumps of berries or grapes are a great way to add a splash of color here and there.

WORK your clump beginning with the darkest color you are using. Make irregular rows of French knots laid very close together. After several rows, begin to work in the second color. If working grapes, narrow the rows to form a roughly triangular shape as you work down toward the point. For clumps or berries, form a more rounded shape. Finally, add the third color to finish. If you are using variegated ribbon, the shading effect will happen as you work without changing ribbon. If you want to emphasize certain areas of the variegated ribbon clump with dark or light, use a matching ribbon color to work in a few extra knots. To finish off your clumps, you may want to add some curlicues of fine silk thread in a stem stitch. Use the stem stitch to attach the clumps to the other parts of the design.

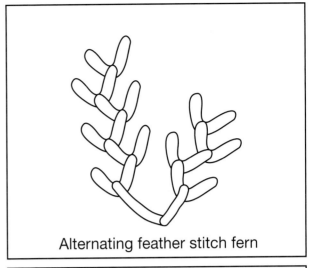

Alternating feather stitch fern

FEATHER STITCH FERNS

Feather stitch ferns are a great filler and finishing touch to any strand or design. They work well in silk thread or silk ribbon. Use a fine silk thread for a delicate feel or silk ribbon for a stronger accent. Either will add movement and a layer of intricacy to any floral design. Dark colors create a dramatic look, while light silvery colors add a feeling of airiness. Since these are final embellishments, they should be worked after the main design is completed. Starting at the top and working toward the bottom minimizes wasted thread or ribbon on the back.

WORK these feather stitch ferns in single or alternating feather stitch, grouped or singly. A variation is to make these ferns with silk ribbon and then add a few straight stitches to the top of each hook with a matching color of silk thread.

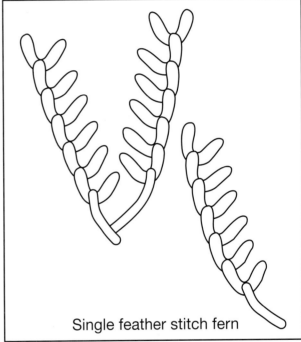

Single feather stitch fern

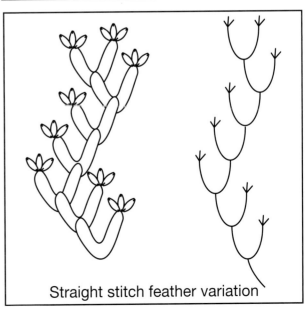

Straight stitch feather variation

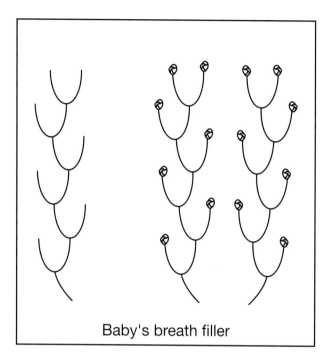

Baby's breath filler

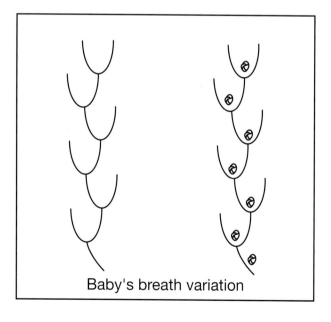

Baby's breath variation

BABY'S BREATH FILLER

When I arrange flowers in a vase, I often add seed pods, dried baby's breath, or bits of ferns for fullness and to finish my arrangement. The same can be done with my favorite stitching filler which I think looks like dried baby's breath. This combination is made with an alternating feather stitch in silk thread, each hook topped off with a silk ribbon French knot. This combination can be used to fill in open areas, add strong contrasting colors, or softly echo the main colors of the work. It creates a subtle and graceful texture change. This filler looks especially good behind roses or other flowers.

WORK this combination in two steps. Working from top to bottom, make several branches of silk thread in alternating feather stitching, coming together at the bottom of the plant. Next take a contrasting color of silk ribbon and top each point of the feather stitch with a French knot.

A variation on this filler is to nestle the French knots down in the curves of the feather stitch instead of on top of the points.

CONE FLOWERS

Those who know me and my work know that I have a special place in my heart for the prairie cone flower. Usually I make it in an appliqué form. But I think making them with ribbon is fun and the cone flower shape adds more variety to my silk embroidery work. These flowers are done with the ribbon stitch and a straight stitch.

WORK the cone flower by first making a thread stem. A little above the stem make three to five ribbon stitches, keeping them pointed roughly downward. With a contrasting ribbon color, make a small top cone with two straight stitches to cross the top of the petals.

DANDELIONS AND FLY STITCH FLOWERS

The fly stitch, worked with ribbon or thread, can be grouped to make a dandelion type of flower or small scattered flowers when done as a single stitch.

WORK a fly stitch dandelion by first making a stem stitch stem in green silk thread. Then above the end of the stem, begin to work extended fly stitches, bringing the thread down to the point of the stem which will become the center of the flower. This will give you a rounded flower. Add French knots in the curves if you wish. To work a single fly stitch flower, begin with some stems and top each one with a small ribbon fly stitch. For variation, use variegated ribbon and stack several fly stitches closely on top of each other.

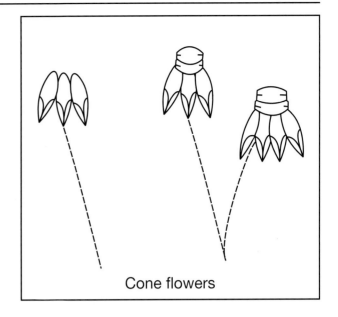

Cone flowers

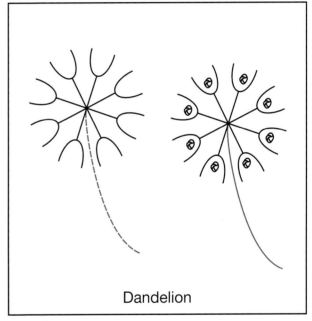

Dandelion

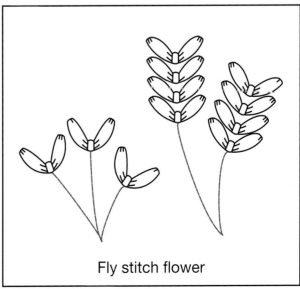

Fly stitch flower

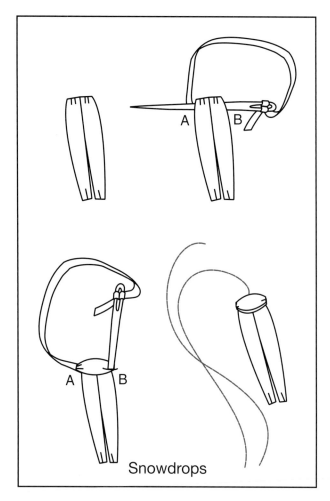

Snowdrops

SNOWDROPS AND HANGING FLOWERS

A hanging flower is another interesting flower shape to add to your work. You can scatter these flowers down a strand of work or group them. They require two colors of ribbon, one for the flower and one for the calyx which should match the stem color.

WORK a snowdrop with a white or cream ribbon. Make two long straight stitches next to each other in a vertical position, keeping your ribbon from twisting. Now take the green ribbon and come up on the left side at the top of your petals. Loop the ribbon above the petals and then go under them on the right side without going into the background. Keep the ribbon from twisting. Now bring the ribbon around to the right side once again and stitch into the background, but do not pull too tightly. This forms the calyx. Finish off with a matching green thread stem to attach the flower to the main design. If you have trouble keeping the ribbon from twisting when you make the straight stitches, do a ribbon stitch instead. This makes a more pointed petal.

Another type of hanging flower can be made with filled lazy daisy stitches positioned so they hang down. Make a group of two or three lazy daisy petals and fill them with a shade of the first ribbon. Then with green ribbon, make a straight stitch across the top end for a calyx and attach the flowers to the main design with green silk thread.

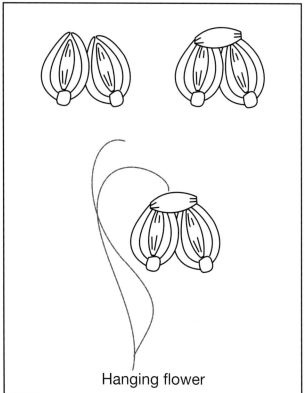

Hanging flower

GRASSES AND SEDGES

I use stalky prairie grasses and sedges (tufted marsh grasses) lavishly in my work. They make a nice compliment to flowers and are good quick fillers. I used to make some grasses from fabric appliqué, but I discovered that I can make them more easily and with more variety with silk ribbon and thread. Grasses tend to grow in clumps and are best portrayed this way. Several grasses originating from the same base will usually be enough to give the effect. Sedges tend to grow in moist areas and vary greatly in size and shape. Here are a few grasses and sedges for you to try.

BIG BLUESTEM is the quintessential prairie grass. It is gold to reddish in color and can be easily made with silk thread and two stitches – chain and stem.

WORK by beginning a stem stitch in silk thread. These grasses wave in the wind and so the stems should curve slightly. Make several side stems which cross the main stem. Repeat so that you have several main stems and side stems without seed heads. Now top the biggest stems with seed heads done in chain stitch using the same silk thread. The seed heads are made of three pieces, the center pieces being slightly longer than the two side ones.

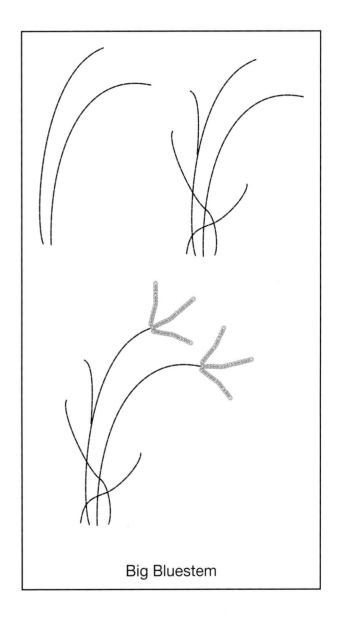

Big Bluestem

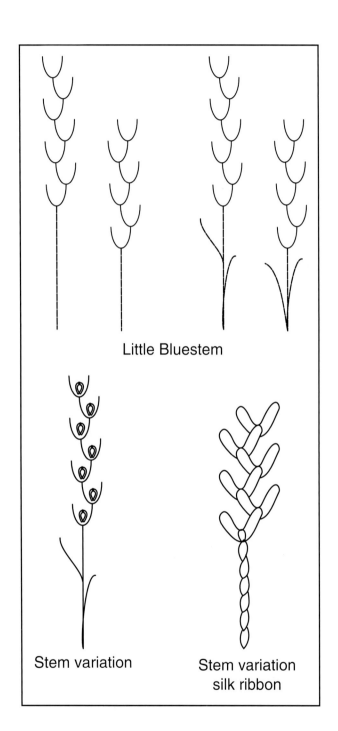

Little Bluestem

Stem variation

Stem variation
silk ribbon

LITTLE BLUESTEM looks quite different and works well in a dark burgundy color. It is made with a stem stitch base and feather stitching to form the seed heads.

WORK top to bottom in silk thread, using the alternating feather stitch to form a seed head. Then switch to a stem stitch – forming straighter stems than the Big Bluestem. Make a main stem for each grass with several side stems without seed heads.

A variation is to go back over the seed head with a slightly different silk thread color, putting a small lazy daisy stitch into each curve of the feather stitch. A second variation for this grass is to make the seed head with silk ribbon in a feather stitch, continuing down with the ribbon to form a stem with the stem stitch.

GRAMMA GRASS is a small grass which can be worked nicely in two colors of silk thread, entirely in the stem stitch. Use a fairly fine silk thread for the best effect.

Work a long, slightly wavy stem stitch stem in the first color. Then make some curly side stems. Off the main stem, work small lines of horizontal stitches on only one side of the main stem, stopping about one-third of the way down the stem. With your second color, work small stem stitch lines of seeds hanging from the horizontal stems.

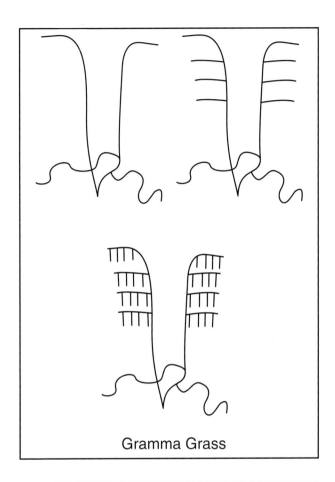

Gramma Grass

PRAIRIE DROP SEED is a good filler grass. I work it in dark colors as a backdrop for other flowers and grasses.

WORK a straight stem with side stems on the top third of the stem, using a dark silk thread. Using the same silk thread, stitch French knots along each of the side stems. From the base, work some extra curved stems which droop to form leaves.

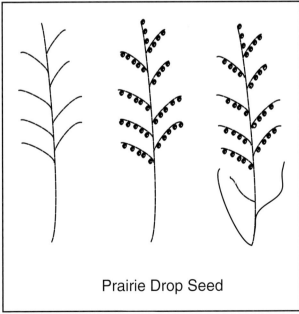

Prairie Drop Seed

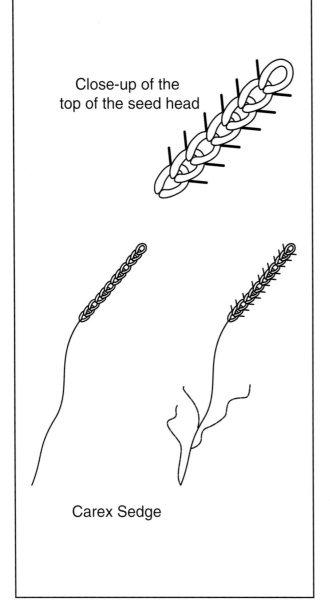

Close-up of the
top of the seed head

Carex Sedge

CAREX SEDGE can be used to suggest a watery place on your quilt, such as the edge of a pond or stream. It has a tight seed head made with silk thread chain stitches and a stem stitch stalk.

WORK the carex sedge from the bottom up with a brown, gold, rust, or sage green silk thread. Begin with a stem stitch to form the stalk, curving gently. Then begin the seed head with a series of chain stitches. At the top of the seed head, work back down to the stalk with the same or a second color of silk thread, looping a straight stitch under the chain stitch to create a spiky look. Make some stem stitch side stalks without seed heads to complete the effect.

There are many other grasses and sedges that you can make using simple stitches. A book of prairie plants, wildflowers, or a botany field guide will show varieties of grasses. I find that books with drawings, rather than photographs, of plants are much more helpful for adapting stitches. Drawings tend to be simpler and less cluttered with background. Refer to the color descriptions of the different grasses you wish to depict for added realism.

FEATHERS, FUR, AND HAIR

Silk ribbon can be used for features such as feathers, fur, and hair that are too difficult to do in appliqué. The French knot will often be your choice for these details. I have seen sheep wool and all types of hair done successfully with French knots.

If you are working on a small *bird*, you may find ribbon will work better to give you feather details than fabric. Larger birds can more easily be portrayed in fabric. How would you best create a row of birds on a wire? They can be quickly done with just a few straight stitches. Flying birds in the distance can be created with a dark ribbon fly stitch grouped in formation. For a small bird with some detail, you may want to appliqué the body of fabric and add details in the ribbon stitch or a straight stitch to create feathers, wings, eyes, beak, legs, and feet.

When working with *fur*, think about the texture and decide on a stitch that best suggests it. Larger animals work fine in fabric. Ribbon is useful for creating a small animal or to add extra depth and detail. A bear is fuzzy and short-furred, so you could use fabric for the bear shape and then add some long straight stitches in silk ribbon of a matching color to suggest the roughness of the fur. Silk ribbon is great for a horse's mane and tail. A rabbit can have pink silk ribbon in his ears and a fluffy white French knot for a tail.

When working on *hair* (page 84), you may use a single color of silk ribbon. However, I find that variegated silk ribbon works especially well as it is hard to shade hair using several different colors and still blend the colors effectively. In working French knots, do not put them in definite rows unless you are trying for a stylized look (e.g., corn rows or a specific style). Do snug them up close to one another as you fill in the area to be covered. You may want first to pencil a light outline of the area to be filled. For long flowing hair, use straight or ribbon stitches. If these stitches are longer than an inch, hold them down with a small silk thread catch stitch or French knot to help prevent snagging.

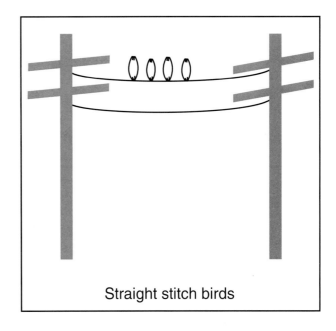

Straight stitch birds

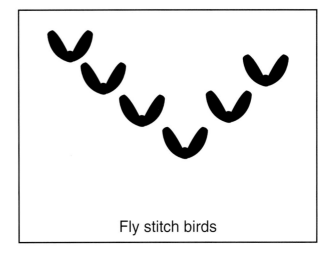

Fly stitch birds

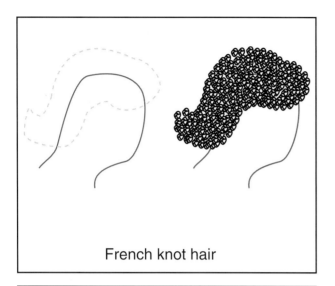

French knot hair

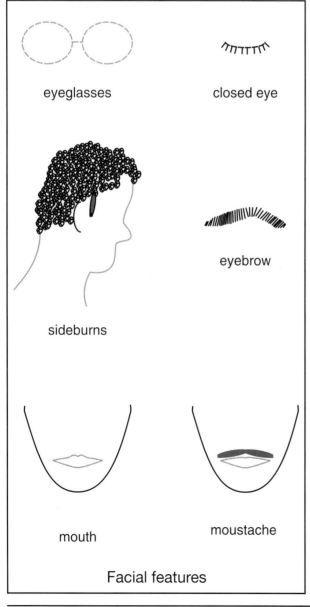

eyeglasses

closed eye

sideburns

eyebrow

mouth

moustache

Facial features

FACIAL FEATURES AND OTHER DETAILS

Small details are often what give character and personality to the living things that populate your quilt, so remember silk ribbons and threads when you need to add those small details. With French knots in ribbon, you can make eyes and noses for animals and humans. Silk thread can create eyebrows, mouths, facial creases, and closed eyes. A straight stitch in ribbon can become a mustache or sideburns, and circles of silver silk thread in a fine outline stitch can create a pair of glasses. Jewelry, birds' legs, and animals' claws can all be made with a few stitches of ribbon. You can give people expression – surprise, contentment, happiness, sadness and sleepiness – with touches of ribbon or thread.

RUFFLES AND FLOURISHES
COUCHED BOWS
AND RIBBONS

A special way to add a touch of fancy to your embellishment is to make silk ribbon bows, streamers, or ruffles. This can be done easily by using a method called "couching." Couching is an embroidery term which simply means "tied down." You tie down the ribbon with small stitches of silk thread, French knots, a running stitch or a line of thread and knots together, such as in a coral stitch.

Note: Couching may not be the best method for clothing that will be washed often because the ribbon may fray more than it would if worked in tighter stitches.

WORK a silk ribbon bow as follows:

1. Thread a 10" to 12" piece of ribbon onto a needle, but do not lock it on or make an end knot.

2. Without catching the background material, slip the needle under the stitching that you wish to embellish, where you want to form your bow.

3. Slip the needle off the ribbon and tie the ribbon into a bow knot with loops. You now have a ribbon bow attached to your piece only at the knot of the bow.

4. Thread an embroidery needle with a matching color of silk thread and knot the end.

5. Begin on one loop of the bow. Make French knots which hold the loop in place. Space the French knots fairly close together – ¼" to ½" apart. As you sew, twist the ribbon after every one or two French knots to change direction. This gives the bow a graceful, interesting shape. Continue on around the entire loop, twisting and shaping the loop as you knot it down, and work back to the bow knot.

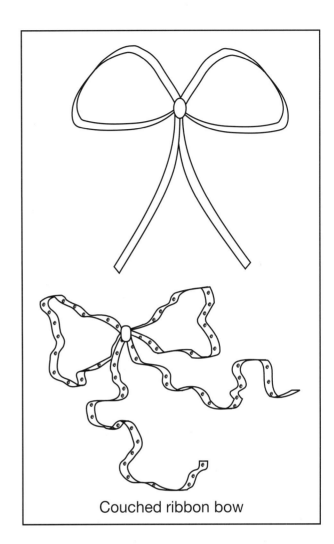

Couched ribbon bow

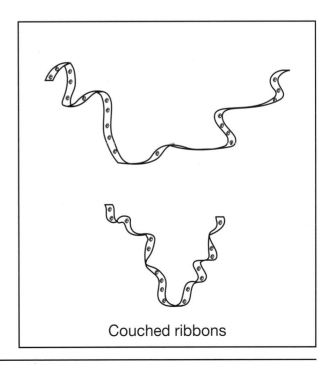

Couched ribbons

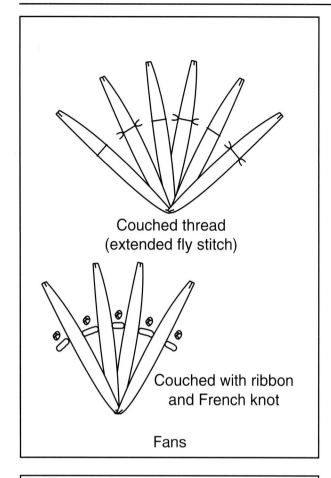

Couched thread
(extended fly stitch)

Couched with ribbon
and French knot

Fans

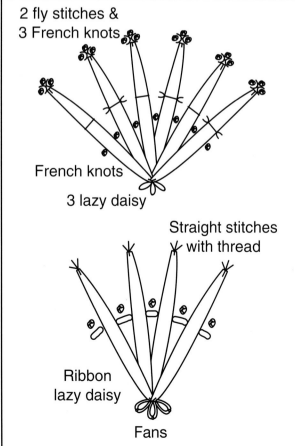

2 fly stitches &
3 French knots

French knots

3 lazy daisy

Straight stitches
with thread

Ribbon
lazy daisy

Fans

6. Continue the same way with the second bow loop.

7. Repeat the same technique with the streamers of the bow, letting them float out and twist as you tie them down with French knots. Use a few small stitches to hold the ends of the streamers down, or tie each ribbon end in a small knot. You may also use a product such as Fray Check to help keep the ends neat.

To make silk ribbon ruffles or streamers, you will use almost the same method as for the bow. Instead of tying a bow, run the needle under some of the completed work to have your ruffle intertwine with the flowers. Then follow steps 4-7 above. Ruffles can be done to add an accent color or to balance your piece. I like sometimes to float ribbons out away from the flowers into the background. Remember to twist the ribbon as you go because the changing direction maximizes the effect of movement.

VARIATIONS AND POSSIBILITIES
Beads can be used for couching instead of French knots. Other good stitches to couch with are the running, chain, and feather stitches. Try using 7 mm silk ribbon for a lush effect. Use a contrasting color of silk thread to tie down the ribbon. Use a variegated ribbon which changes color as it twists.

FANS AND MEDALLIONS

Fans and medallions add interest to any crazy quilt work that you do. A fan is a quarter, third, or half circle of stitches, while a medallion is a complete circle of stitches. Couching with silk ribbon works well for fans and medallions. Many of the spokes of your fans or medallions can be worked with a long straight stitch of ribbon. You can then tie down those spokes with silk thread or ribbon in a contrasting color. Combining thread and ribbon gives more visual texture and possibilities for great color combinations.

Fans and medallions look quite complex, and can be made of an endless variety of easy stitch combinations. Remember that a fan can continue around to become a medallion. Consider using medallions on clothing, in the center of a piece for the main focal point, along borders and especially with fans in a linear fashion to emphasize a line on your quilt. Pictures of old crazy quilts can give you lots of ideas.

Note: In the illustrations shown on page 86, the thicker lines represent ribbon while the thin lines represent thread.

WORK fans from a lightly marked center point. You may also need to mark dots for the outer circle at first, but work at learning to eyeball your stitches to make them approximately even. To begin a fan, make six long (about 1½") straight stitches from the same center hole covering about one-third of a circle. You will want some space between the ribbon to add other decorative stitches. Now couch these stitches down with thread using one of the methods shown in top drawing of top illustration on page 86.

Now add a few stitches at the top of the fan and also at the base. Some examples you can try are shown in top drawing of bottom illustration on page 86. These are worked with thread.

To further embellish the fan, add some French knots in ribbon or lazy daisies in thread or ribbon. Change colors often. Consider working a fan sampler to capture some of your ideas for use later. Almost all the stitches explained in this chapter can be used to create fans.

WORK medallions much the same way as fans, but complete the circle. You may choose to make them symmetrically or not. You can add center

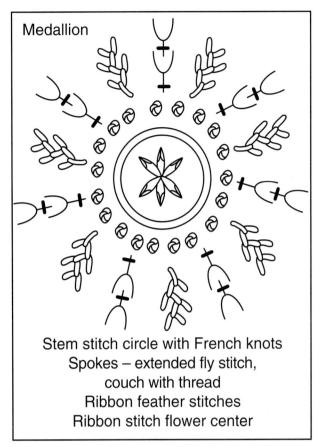

Medallion

Stem stitch circle with French knots
Spokes – extended fly stitch,
couch with thread
Ribbon feather stitches
Ribbon stitch flower center

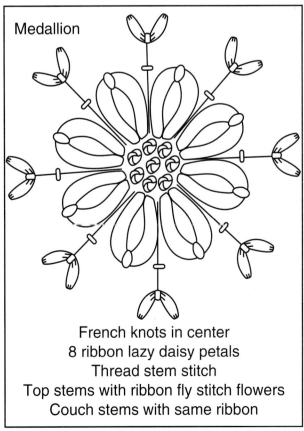

Medallion

French knots in center
8 ribbon lazy daisy petals
Thread stem stitch
Top stems with ribbon fly stitch flowers
Couch stems with same ribbon

stitches if you wish. To begin, lightly pencil in a circle. Then stitch both inside and outside the circle. There is no one correct size, but vary the height of your medallions to keep the eye moving. The illustrations on the previous page will give you some ideas to try. For example, you could couch down silk thread with the ribbon for a lacy delicate effect.

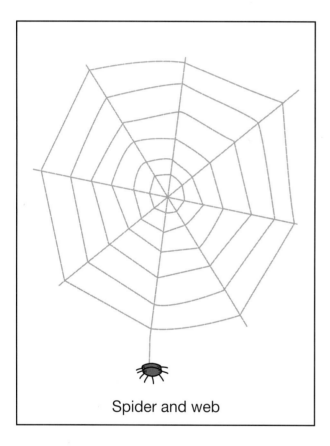

Spider and web

SPIDER WEBS AND SPIDERS

I like to populate my quilts with various fauna found in nature and one of my favorite additions is a spider web. Recently a group of kids looking at one of my quilts with a spider web on it asked where the spider was, so now I add a spider to each web. A silver metallic thread adds special glitz to your web.

WORK a spider web using a stem stitch in silver or other metallic thread. Make the spokes first and then stitch the connecting webbing. Make the base or spokes of the web with four stem stitch lines that cross in the center. Do not place them at exactly 90° to each other, but vary the angles for a more natural look. Then begin near the center and make stem stitch connecting strands, curving them slightly toward the center. Continue around until you have connected the spokes in a rough circle, and then make the next rows of connecting stitches. If you have nestled your web among flowers and leaves, be sure the ends of the spokes attach to them, just as they would in nature.

WORK a spider hanging down from the end of a stem stitch thread with two small horizontal straight stitches in a dark color silk ribbon. Place these stitches on top of each other to form the body. With a fine thread, work eight small legs hanging down from the spider body – a few stem stitches for each leg. If you want the spider to be on the web, work the body the same way, locating it somewhere on the web. Instead of hanging the legs down, extend them out from the body, four on each side. Don't worry about eyes or other features because the body and legs will be enough to give the impression of a spider.

Chapter 6

BUILDING A STRAND

"The result of every operation during productions is determined by the workman as he works and its outcome depends wholly or largely on his care, judgment and dexterity."

David Pye – *The Nature and Art of Workmanship*

INTRODUCTION

Building a strand of embroidered flowers is a learning exercise, to practice using the ribbons and threads, as well as learning some of the stitches. You will find it easier to add silk ribbon embellishment to your appliqué and patchwork once you are comfortable handling the ribbon and working the stitches.

Some of the projects in the next two chapters use this strand technique as the major design element. By doing some of them you will become much more at ease handling the ribbon and stitches as well as better understand the layering idea I present here in detail. It is my hope that you will also begin to use this idea to design with silk ribbon and make it a permanent fixture in your embellishment repertoire.

HOW TO BUILD A STRAND USING SILK RIBBON AND THREAD

This technique teaches you the basics for working with floral layered designs of any sort. After you master the idea of building up the layers to create a finished "strand" of flowers, stems, and leaves, you will be able to adapt this idea to stitch endless combinations of flowers.

The idea behind building a strand of flowers is to add new stitches or colors each time you go over the original design. The final design will look very complex, but has actually been built up gradually from simple stitches. Once you understand how to layer and combine your stitches and colors, you will find that building a strand is merely a jumping off point. A strand can be the focal point of a piece, used as a background detail, or it can add occasional touches of color.

To learn to build a strand we will follow six steps, adding a color or different stitch each time. To begin, I suggest building a straight strand. Remember, this is a step-by-step procedure and will not look finished until the last embellishments, so don't be discouraged by the look of this piece as you work through the steps. Be sure to pick some interesting flower colors and add some extra zing with your two accent colors.

Materials:
- Piece of plain muslin
- 6" embroidery hoop (round or oval)
- Chenille needles for the ribbon
- Embroidery needle for the silk thread
- Assorted 4 mm silk ribbon in the following colors:
    3 greens
    3 flower colors
    2 accent colors
- Silk thread in two accent colors (e.g., green and brown or gold and dark red)

Stitches:
Feather – alternating and single
Detached twisted chain
Ribbon stitch
French knot
Couched bow

Begin by positioning your muslin and tightening the hoop. Lock one of the green silk ribbons on your chenille needle and you are ready to begin.

STEP 1 – Lay down a base of feather stitches, which will be the foundation for the rest of the stitches, leaving room at the top above the feather stitching for the flowers. This base defines the shape of the finished garland or bouquet. You may draw a straight line to follow if you wish, but it is best to learn to do your feather stitches by eye. Work top to bottom to minimize wasting ribbon on the back of your piece. For this example, try to work within the hoop so that you do not have to reposition it. Knot off the ribbon on the back.

STEP 2 – With a second green, add leaves using a detached twisted chain stitch. Begin at the bottom of the strand and work up to minimize wasted thread on the back. Lay each stitch between the feather stitching "hooks" as shown in the illustration below.

You now have two colors of leaves in two styles of stitching and are ready to add the third green to further fill in the strand.

STEP 3 – This third green is done in the ribbon stitch. Work it from bottom to top of the strand to minimize wasted ribbon on the back. Let some of these stitches cross the feather stitch base to further blend the colors of the leaves. Add ribbon stitch leaves to both sides of the strand, but do not work them too tightly in order to leave some space for the next step, adding flowers.

STEP 4 – In this simplified example you will add flowers using only the detached twisted chain stitch. Because you will be using flower colors, this stitch will look quite different from the green used earlier for the leaves. This time begin about one-third of the way up from the bottom and add the flowers to the outer edge of the strand. Keep them on the edge, but close enough to the leaves so they do not float out away from the strand. You will want to work up each side of the strand, leaving room between the flowers for all three flower colors. Put a few across the top of the strand to give it a rounded effect.

Repeat over the same part of the strand with the second flower color. Put these just above or just below the first flowers. Do not space them too regularly, but group them in small groups, blending with the leaves and previous flowers.

STEP 5 – Now add the third flower color, again using the detached twisted chain stitch. You can

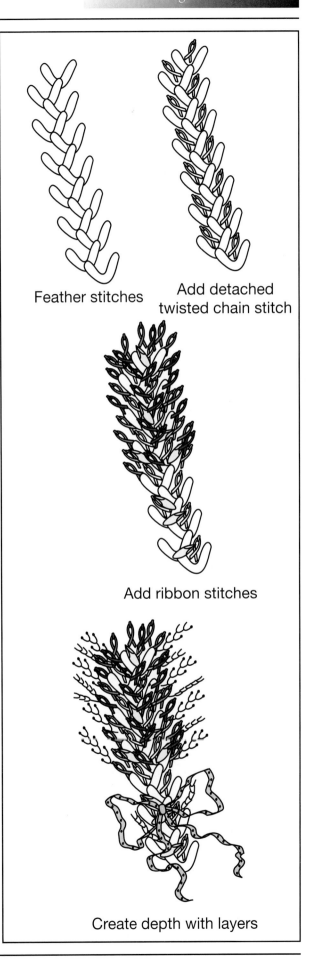

Feather stitches

Add detached twisted chain stitch

Add ribbon stitches

Create depth with layers

lighten or darken the whole strand with this color or you can add a new color to accent the flowers you have already made. Put a few of these flowers along the spine of the strand to help give a feeling of depth.

STEP 6 – Now you are ready to embellish the strand with some silk thread. Begin with one color of silk thread at the top of your piece. Using the alternating feather stitch, work some ferns down the strand as far as the flowers on each side.

Now top each of the points of the feather stitching with a French knot in one of your accent colors of silk ribbon. This effect of baby's breath adds a lot of appeal and another shot of color to your strand. With your second color of silk thread, add some single feather stitch ferns between the completed baby's breath. This looks best done with a finer silk thread and can continue the full length of the strand on both sides.

STEP 7 (optional) – You are ready to add a couched bow to finish off the strand. Take your second accent ribbon and follow the couching directions in Chapter 5. Be sure to turn and twist the ribbon as you tie it down with the French knots. This can be a bow or just a floating ribbon across the piece. See some of the strand variations for ways to place this ribbon.

VARIATIONS

You can use this technique of building a strand in a myriad of ways in your own work. The key is the first stitches that you lay down which give direction to the rest of the piece. You can use a wavy line of feather stitching, a curved line, a closed or open circle or a heart shape, to name just a few possibilities.

For the sake of simplicity, this example was limited to flower stitches, but you can build a strand with a great variety of flowers including roses, bunches of grapes, branches of blossoms, or leaves. The combination stitches shown in Chapter 5 can be a starting place, and as you try them, you will probably come up with your own ideas.

Once you have built a few strands of your own, you will have the experience to do them your own way, adding stitches and colors that you like.

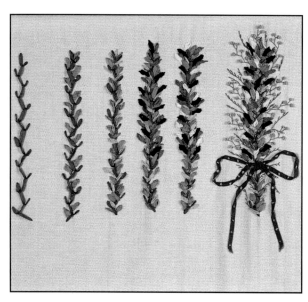

Building a strand.

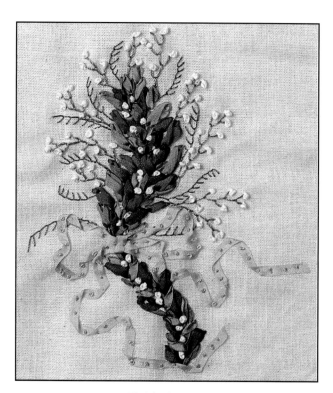

Finished strand.

Chapter 7

PRACTICE PROJECTS

"Lucy Locket lost her pocket,
Kitty Fisher found it;
Nothing in it, nothing in it
But the binding round it."

Mother Goose

INTRODUCTION

The golden age of embroidery ended about the time the American Revolution began. Up until that time, many household goods including those used by men were embroidered in some manner. The two small projects included in this chapter are based on eighteenth-century items I studied in museum collections. Student interest from classes I teach convinced me that these two items still have a lot of appeal to stitchers today.

You can make them for their historic interest, for practicing silk ribbon embroidery, and to create items that are both useful and beautiful. Either of these items makes a thoughtful gift from those of us who still ply a needle in this computer age.

COLONIAL POCKET

In the eighteenth century, women did not have pockets sewn into their clothing. Instead they wore pear-shaped cloth bags which tied around their waists. These "pockets" had a slit so that you could reach inside to get items kept there. Women kept things in their pockets such as sewing notions, keys, and small personal items. Pockets were often made in pairs and worn under their petticoats (skirts) for security. They were made out of linen or a sturdy cotton, sometimes printed and sometimes plain.

Pockets could also be decorated with embroidery. Embroidered pockets were most often worn over the petticoats. Tradition says young unmarried women would often do their best embroidery on their pockets and then wear them on the outside of their clothing as a subtle way to advertise their homemaking skills.

Pockets went out of style as fashion changed at the end of the eighteenth century. Styles became slimmer and the bulk of a pocket became undesirable. Women then carried pockets or pocketbooks which were also often decorated with embroidery or bead work.

Today making a pocket to tie around your waist is right in fashion, considering the popularity of fannypacks. The following design is for a sewing pocket based on the eighteenth-century English style. I assure you if you make this and decorate it with silk ribbon embroidery, you will get admiration and attention when you wear it at your next quilt show – although that will probably come from other quilters, not from men in buckskins.

TO MAKE A POCKET

Materials:
- ½ yard of bleached or unbleached muslin
- Optional piece of interfacing or thin muslin to cover the back side of the embroidery
- 1½ to 2 yards of twill tape or grosgrain ribbon to attach and tie around the waist
- Cardboard or template plastic

Assorted silk ribbons:
Three greens to build a strand
Two to three flower colors
Two accent colors
Silk thread for decorative stitching

Begin your pocket by making a cardboard or plastic template of the pattern on page 97. Trace two pocket shapes on your muslin and one on the interfacing or lining material (optional). Mark the slit position on one pocket lightly in pencil. This will be the front of your pocket on which you will do your embellishment. Complete the embroidery before trimming this piece to help retain its shape.

Position the front of the pocket on your hoop and with one green silk ribbon begin your strand. You may want to curve it around to follow the line of the pocket. Another possibility is to leave a space for a spider web rose near the base. Work the three greens into a strand using the feather, detached twisted chain, and ribbon stitches.

Next, work in one or two flower colors using the detached twisted chain stitch, and a rose at the base if you desire. Embellish your strand with silk thread feather stitching topped with silk ribbon French knots.

Remove the hoop, trim both pieces of the pocket and lining, leaving a ½" seam allowance. Lay the front of your pocket with the wrong side to the lining and stitch around the edge. Carefully cut along the pencil line you marked earlier for the slit through both the pocket and lining fabrics. Now blindstitch the slit of the pocket, rolling a narrow seam to the inside over the lining.

Next, attach the back of the pocket by placing it over the stitched side of the front (right sides together) and stitching completely around the edge. Turn the pocket through the slit.

Finally, to make a casing for hanging the pocket on your grosgrain ribbon or twill tape, turn the top edge of the pocket to the back and blind stitch it down. Slip your ribbon or tape through the casing. If you wish, you may also put a line of quilting ½" in from the edge of the pocket to help cover the raw edge inside.

Pocket (above) and Pocket detail (below left). Cathy Grafton.

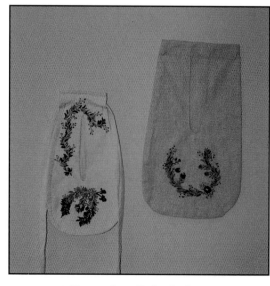

Two pockets. Cathy Grafton.

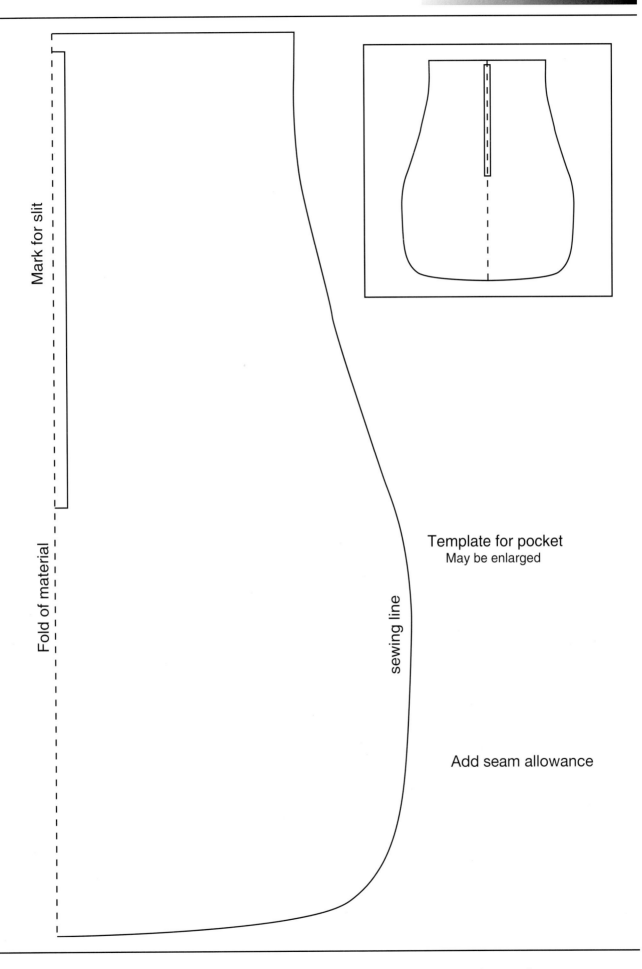

Mark for slit

Fold of material

sewing line

Template for pocket
May be enlarged

Add seam allowance

"The sailor, with long months or even years at sea, had his own characteristic sewing tools which he carried in his ditty-bag or box. A rolled-up hussif contained needles, thimble and hanks of thread for mending, darning and sewing on buttons. His pincushion, made most likely by his wife or sweetheart, was probably heart-shaped, with 'Good Luck' pricked out in pins and colored beads — a mascot to bring him back safely from his voyage."

Sylvia Groves – *The History of Needlework Tools and Accessories*

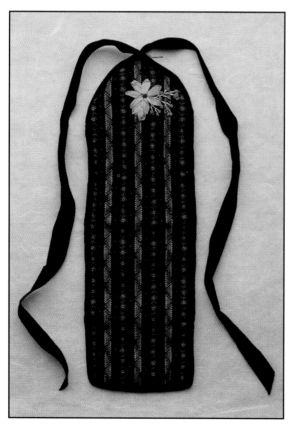

Open houswife. Cathy Grafton.

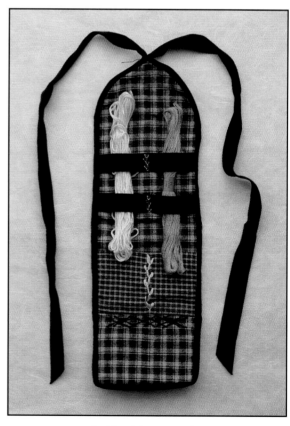

Inside of the houswife.

18TH CENTURY HOUSEWIFE
Sewing Kit

The houswife project is a favorite in my classes. Though you may never have heard of a "housewife," you may want to try one.

A "housewife" (huswif, housewif, hussif or huzzif variously in dialect) was a small portable sewing kit that men often took on journeys such as hunting trips or when going off to war. It held hanks of thread, needles, pins, beeswax, and perhaps an extra horn button. Some form of these portable sewing kits was carried by sailors, hunters, and soldiers from the French and Indian War to the Revolutionary and Civil wars and even into World War I. They changed from cloth to leather as time passed, but were still used for the same purpose – mending while far from home.

These housewives were decorated with embroidery or left plain, depending on the skill and time of the seamstress. Older ones often show evidence of careful choices of fabrics with small pockets or bands sewn on the inside to hold threads and sewing items.

This pattern is based on a design from the eighteenth century, but can be as handy today to carry your sewing notions. Of course this one will be embellished with silk ribbon designs, which would have probably been a little delicate for the average soldier, but they are a great way to attract attention today. You can keep items inside such as needles, pins, threads, a thimble, beeswax, scissors (cover the point), a bodkin, buttons, and a tape measure.

TO MAKE A HOUSEWIFE

Materials:
- 3 or more print or solid scraps of fabric for front and lining (fat quarters are a good choice)
- A 60" piece of ½" black twill tape for binding and the ties
- Assorted colors of silk ribbon and thread for decorating
- A piece of batting 3" x 4" for the pincushion area

You can sew your housewife by hand as in the eighteenth century or use a sewing machine.

Cut two fabric rectangles 4" x 12" from two of your scrap colors. The outer fabric should be plain or a subtle print, not too busy so it will be suitable for decorating with silk ribbon. The lining fabric can be any type of print. The third color is for making a pocket and fabric bands to hold thread and other items.

There are several suggestions on page 101 for embellishing the outside with silk ribbon work.

The houswife closed and tied.

Assembly diagram for sewing kit

Flip after sewing

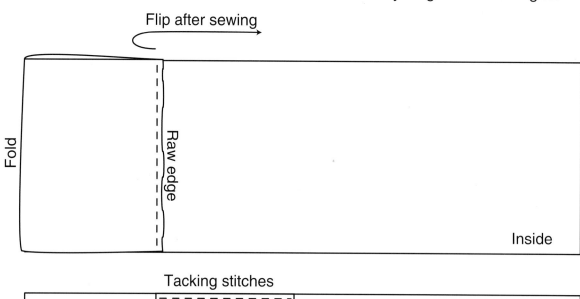

Fold

Raw edge

Inside

Tacking stitches

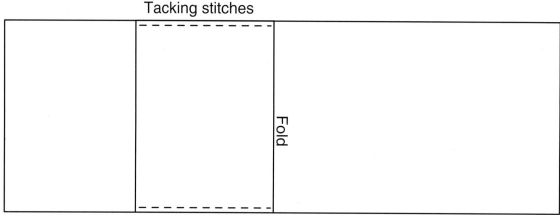

Fold

Add decorative stitching here

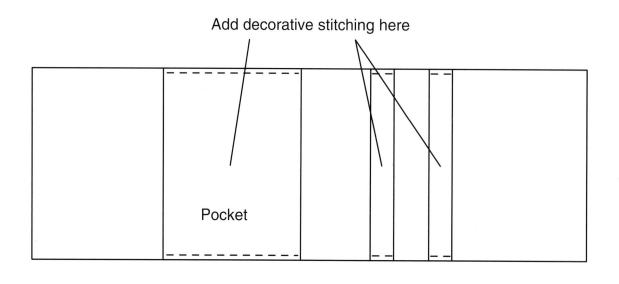

Pocket

Design suggestions for embellishing
the outside of the sewing kit

These are for a simple decorated flower and leaf design, or you may want to design your own. Do the embroidery at one end of the outer fabric rectangle about 1½" from the end. Set the outside rectangle aside after you have embroidered it.

Attach the pocket and bands to the lining before putting the two pieces together. From your third color scraps, cut a 4" x 6" piece for the pocket. Fold it in half to give you a 4" x 3" piece. Place the fold along one end of the lining rectangle so that the raw edge lies about one-quarter of the way up on the right side. Now machine or hand-stitch the raw edge to the lining with a ¼" seam. Flip the pocket over the seam to cover the raw edge. Tack it on each side edge with a few stitches ⅛" from the lining edge.

To make the bands which will hold embroidery thread or silk ribbon, cut a 1½" x 8" strip from the pocket or third color fabric. Sew this strip together, right sides out, with a ¼" seam. Now cut this strip in half to get two ½" x 4" pieces and iron the seam to the backside. Position one strip 1½" above the pocket and the second ¾" above the first. Tack it along each side.

Now you are ready to do some decorative silk thread stitching to help hold these pieces down onto the lining. This stitching can be done up the center of the pocket and at the center of each strip (see photo). There are a variety of small stitches you can use here, such as the feather stitch and chain stitch. You may want to add a few French knots of silk ribbon as well.

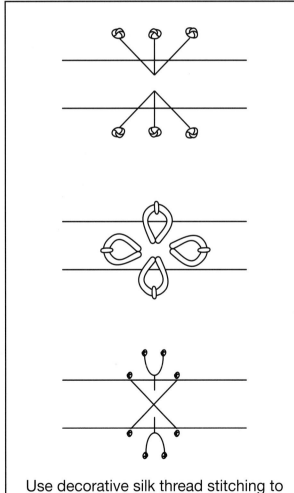

Use decorative silk thread stitching to
hold the pieces down onto the lining

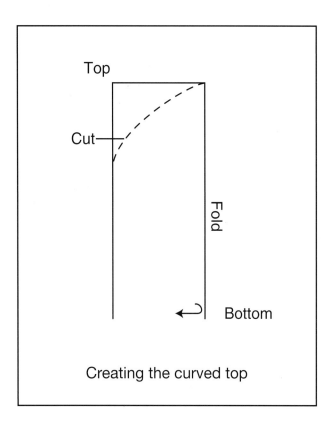

Creating the curved top

To finish your housewife, place the two rectangles together with the right sides facing out. Place the outside piece with the flower at the top end. Fold them lengthwise in toward the lining and cut a slightly rounded shape or a point at the end of the top rectangle, being careful not to cut into your flower design. Unfold the pieces. Next place the batting scrap between the two rectangles at the bottom end of your housewife, below the pocket, and pin them together.

Now, measure 10" of the twill tape for the ties. Leave them loose. Starting at the top of the rounded end, pin the tape to the entire raw edge on the outside, matching the edges. Stitch from the rounded edge all the way around back to the other side of the rounded edge using a ¼" seam. The extra tape will hang loose as the second tie piece.

Flip the tape over the raw edge and blindstitch it to the lining to cover the raw edges. Use the two strings at the rounded edge to tie your housewife closed.

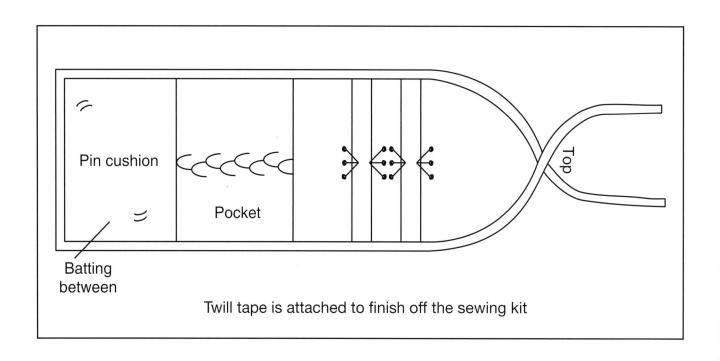

Twill tape is attached to finish off the sewing kit

Chapter 8

SILK RIBBON SAMPLERS AND SMALL QUILTS

"The sampler was originally a cloth used to practice stitches and stitch combinations. It was also a means of learning to execute embroidery patterns and designs."

Glee Krueger – *A Gallery of American Samplers*

INTRODUCTION

This final section of the book contains ideas for creating samplers, including small banners, quilted wallhangings, runners, and pictorial pieces. They are simple pieces to help you practice your stitches and give you a chance to adapt and design if you wish. Some involve piecing and some appliqué, but all are on a small, manageable scale.

I strongly urge you to add your own flower combinations and color choices. I have given you a framework to work within, so you have some limits already set. Coming up with your own ideas should be quite feasible – holidays, special events, seasonal decorating needs, or just for fun. After doing some of these samplers, you will have the skill to begin to add silk ribbon to your wallhangings and larger quilts.

QUILTING YOUR SAMPLERS

I think it best to keep the quilting fairly simple on most of these projects. I usually quilt around the main designs but avoid quilting on top of any silk ribbon stitching. Sometimes I also choose a simple grid of diamonds or squares to fill the background areas. On more elaborate appliqué or pieced samplers, you can work out other quilting designs that please you.

For most of these samplers I suggest binding them by bringing the backing over the front to form a ½" binding. These samplers are lightweight and will not strain a simple binding like a larger quilt might. In most cases, after binding is completed, I also stitch a row of quilting just inside the binding.

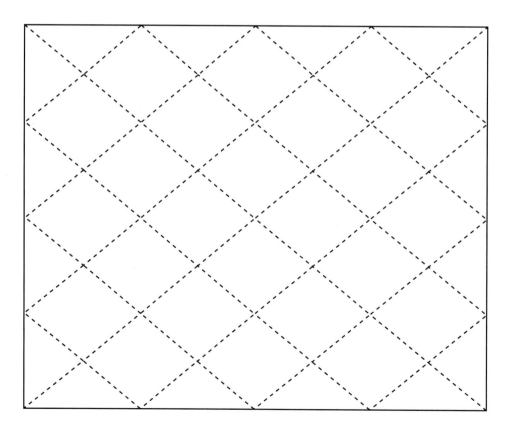

Example of quilting in a diamond pattern.

HANGING YOUR SAMPLERS
(Invisible Wire Method)

Since many of these samplers are small, I have developed a way to hang them without framing. This method stiffens the tops of the samplers with a wire insert so they will hang without drooping in the middle. This method works well on lightweight samplers and banners. However, I don't recommend it for anything larger. You will need the following items to do this technique.

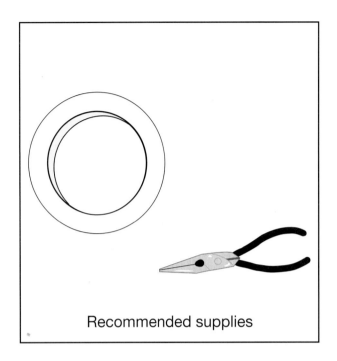

Recommended supplies

Materials:
- ▶ 16 gauge florist wire
  (available at your local florist shop)
- ▶ Wire cutter
- ▶ Masking tape

As you bind off your sampler, leave the top binding to sew last so that you can insert the wire. I often bring the backing over the front to bind or you may add a separate binding fabric if you desire. Either way, remember to leave the top binding unsewn to allow inserting the wire in the next step.

Cut a piece of the wire ½" shorter than the length of the top of your piece. Cut the wire with wire cutters (not your best scissors, please) and cover the rough edges on each end with masking tape to prevent damage to the fabric binding.

Lay the wire just inside the top binding and blindstitch the binding down, enclosing the wire. The wire holds the piece rigid across the top for hanging, but is invisible. If need be at a later date, the wire can always be removed by loosening the top binding and slipping it out.

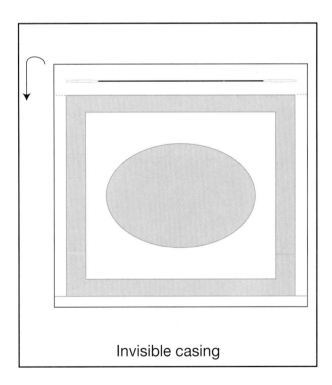

Invisible casing

For hanging, sew a casing along the top of the reverse side of the piece and run a rod through it, or use my favorite method which is to crochet a piece of silk ribbon, pearl cotton or glitzy novelty thread to attach for hanging. Sew the ribbon on at each end on the back and you are ready to hang your sampler.

Holidays

ABOVE: Merry Merry Christmas. Cathy Grafton.
BELOW: Merry Merry Christmas detail.

ABOVE: Keep Christmas. Cathy Grafton.
BELOW: Keep Christmas detail.

SEWING NOTIONS

For each of these projects, you will need sewing notions, including your needles – chenille, embroidery and quilting – scissors, pencils, thimble, and other threads that might be needed for binding, making a base for spider web roses, and quilting. See Chapter 3 for more information on notions and tools, if necessary.

HOLIDAYS
Hanukkah and Christmas

If you don't have time to make a large wallhanging for an upcoming holiday, consider making a small sampler to hang on a door or inside your house to add to the festive atmosphere. Using similar styles, you can make a sampler for Christmas, Hanukkah or any special holiday.

MAKING A HANUKKAH SAMPLER

Because our family has celebrated Hanukkah for years with our friends Bruce and Linda Unterman, we are familiar with many of its customs and traditions. I thought it would be nice to make them this special sampler for Hanukkah. You can use the Star of David, a Menorah or another symbol that is special to your own celebration of this Jewish holiday.

Materials:
- ▸ 9" x 9" piece of linen or muslin for top
- ▸ 9" x 9" piece of batting
- ▸ 9" x 9" piece of cotton print for backing – blue, yellow, gold, white are color suggestions
- ▸ Assorted silk ribbons:
    three greens for leaves on the strand
    dark blue or burgundy for the flowers
    accent colors for the rose and French knots
- ▸ Silk threads
    for the star or other symbol
    accent colors for feather stitching
- ▸ Pearl cotton or novelty thread for lettering

Hanukkah Sampler. Cathy Grafton.

Hanukkah Sampler detail..

On your background fabric, mark an 8" x 8" square. Lightly pencil in the word "Hanukkah" two-thirds of the way down the square. Above and to the left pencil in your star or other Hanukkah symbol.

Put the fabric in your hoop. Stitch the lettering with a stem stitch and pearl cotton or other heavy thread. Stitch the lines of the star with an outline stitch in blue silk thread.

Below the "H" in "Hanukkah," make a spider web rose using one of your accent colors of silk ribbon. Embellish the rose with single feather stitches in silk thread.

Now build three strands down to the rose as shown below. The one on the left will be taller.

The two on the right will just touch the bottom of the star. Work through the lettering, trying not to obscure it. Work the strand with feather, detached twisted chain, and ribbon stitches in your three green colors. Go back over the strand with your main flower color, adding flowers in the detached twisted chain stitch. Embellish the strands with silk thread feather stitching topped with silk ribbon French knots.

Remove the hoop, trim your square, add batting and the backing, and do some simple quilting around the main design elements. Bind and use the invisible wire method (page 105). Add a line of quilting just inside the binding to finish.

Placement for Hanukkah sampler

MAKING A CHRISTMAS SAMPLER

I have used "Merry Merry Christmas" on my Christmas sampler. However, you can use "Merry Christmas," "Keep Christmas," "Noel," "Feliz Navidad" or any holiday greeting that you desire.

Materials:
- ▶ 11" x 11" piece of linen or muslin for the top
- ▶ Scrap of dark green print fabric for tree and brown print for trunk
- ▶ Fat quarters or scraps of red and green print fabric for strip pieced border
- ▶ 14" x 14" piece of batting for filling
- ▶ 14" x 14" piece of cotton print for backing – a good place to use a Christmas fabric
- ▶ Assorted silk ribbons:
    three greens for leaves on strand
    red (variegated if possible) and plum for flowers
    accent colors for ribbon and tree trim
- ▶ Silk thread for tree trim, lettering and feather stitching on the strand
- ▶ Pearl cotton or glitzy novelty thread for some of the lettering

On your background fabric mark a 10" x 10" square. To cut out the evergreen tree, fold the green fabric and cut free-hand or trace the tree pattern on page 110. Appliqué the tree in the lower left corner of your sampler, adding a small trunk with your brown fabric.

With a pencil lightly write in "Merry Merry," centered, and about one-third of the way down the square. Write in "Christmas" below that and to the right of the tree. Put your fabric on your hoop and embroider the lettering using a stem stitch. Use pearl cotton or novelty thread for "Merry

Merry" and a strong color of regular silk thread to embroider "Christmas."

In the upper right hand corner build a three-part strand using your green silk ribbon colors and the same strand stitches you have been using – feather, detached twisted chain, and ribbon stitch. (Check the photo for positioning.) You want your strand to come up to the lettering without obscuring it. Add a few flowers to the strand with a strong plum or burgundy silk ribbon using the detached twisted chain stitch.

Now, add stems along the strand in silk thread – about three for each strand. Next, up and down each side of the stems, work French knots in your red silk ribbon. The red will look more dramatic if you use a variegated ribbon.

You may want to couch a ribbon entwined in the strand to add another touch of color. I used a cream 7 mm ribbon, or you may use 4 mm. See the instructions on couching in Chapter 5.

Now it is time to trim the tree! In this exercise I used a coral stitch for both of the garlands – the gold is done with silk thread and the red with silk ribbon which gives two very different looks using the same stitch. Add a few ornaments using French knots, fly stitch flowers, and cross stitch flowers. Top the tree with a ribbon stitch star. Remove the hoop and trim the piece.

For the border, strip piece together several red and green prints. Then cut 2½" wide borders and sew those into place on each side of the central block. Mark a 1" diagonal grid lightly with a chalk pencil for quilting. Place on top of the batting and backing, and quilt. Do not quilt through the strand or the tree. Outline quilt along the strip-pieced seams of the border or use a quilting design of your choice.

To finish, bind by bringing the back over the front or cut a separate binding. Use the invisible wire method (page 105) to stiffen the piece for hanging.

Christmas Sampler

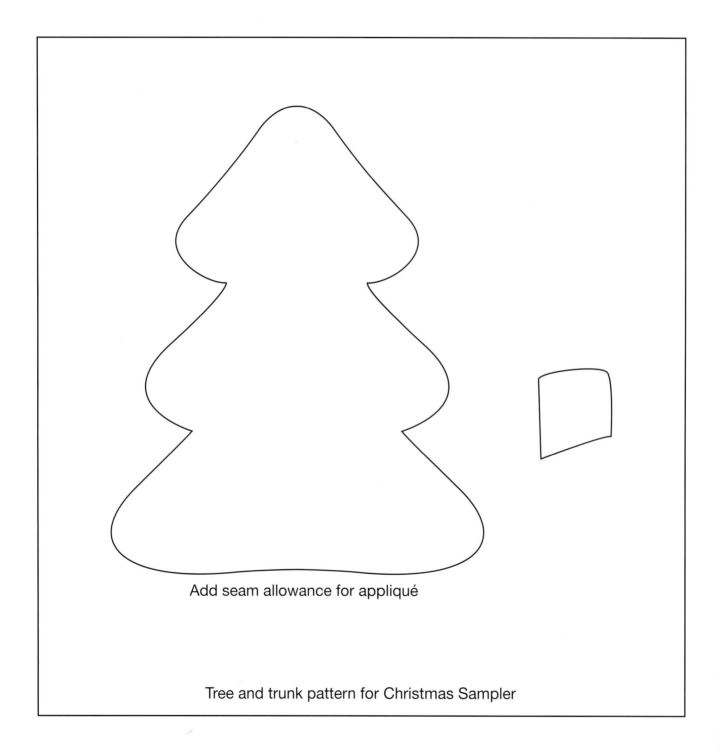

Add seam allowance for appliqué

Tree and trunk pattern for Christmas Sampler

Dee's Cocina. Cathy Grafton.

Dee's Cocina detail.

Dee's Cocina

FRIENDSHIP
Dee's Cocina

Giving gifts you have made yourself to friends allows you to personalize them in a unique way. I like to make small banners or samplers for friends. This example is a simple one that could also be done for rooms other than the kitchen. My friend Dee is a good cook and loves to make ethnic foods.

MAKING A KITCHEN SAMPLER

If your friend likes certain ethnic foods or is from an ethnic background, it is nice to use a foreign language for the word "kitchen." For example, "cocina" is Spanish for kitchen, "cucina" is Italian, "kuche" or "kuchen" is German. Or you can use a cooking phrase for the type of food that is your friend's specialty.

> Materials:
> ▶ 10" x 10" piece of linen or muslin for top
> ▶ 10" x 10" piece of batting for filling
> ▶ 10" x 10" piece of cotton print for backing
> ▶ Assorted silk ribbons:
>   three greens for leaves on strand
>   several flower colors
>   accent colors for couched ribbon and trim
> ▶ Silk thread for decorative feather stitches and lettering

On your background fabric, mark off an 8" x 8" square. With a pencil, lightly write in the words you wish to embroider two-thirds of the way down the square. Below that, pencil in a half-oval which starts and ends along each side of the lettering.

Put the fabric in your hoop and on the top two-thirds of your marked square, build two strands with your green silk ribbon. Use the building a strand method (see Chapter 6) with the feather stitch, detached twisted chain, and ribbon stitch in all three greens. Work the strands so they come together about 2" to 3" above the lettering. Refer to the picture on page 111 for placement or adapt as you desire.

Where the strands come together, work a spider web rose in one of your flower colors. To one side of the rose, work a small strand in the three greens using the same stitches. You can work a second smaller rose in another color if you wish.

On all three strands, work a few hanging flowers in a second flower color. Attach these to the strands with silk thread. Finally, embellish the strands with single feather stitching. Below the rose, work two small strands with your three greens. Then, using one of your accent colors, couch a small ribbon floating over them. Tie a knot in the middle of this piece of ribbon and remember to twist it to change directions as you couch it down with thread French knots.

Work the lettering you have marked in a fine silk thread in chain stitch. Follow your pencil lines on the oval with a single, very open feather stitch in silk ribbon. In between each feather, put a French knot – this is a good place to use variegated silk ribbon to get a lot of color worked into the French knots. Top each end of the oval with three ribbon stitches and a French knot.

Remove the hoop, trim your square, add the batting and backing, and do some simple quilting around the main design elements. Bind the edges and use the invisible wire method (page 105) to hang the piece. Add a line of quilting just inside the binding to finish.

ABOVE: Crazy quilt runner. Cathy Grafton.
BELOW: Crazy quilt runner details.

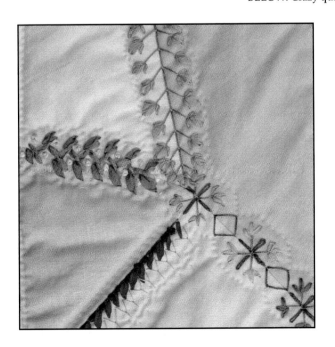 

PIECED SAMPLER
Crazy quilt runner

This can be a true sampler of all the stitches you have learned. What makes it charming is a good blend of silk threads and ribbons. Work different stitches in the same color, or with a variety of both colors and stitches. I chose pastel and cream colored fabrics for this background, but it would be quite effective to use a more traditional darker background as well.

MAKING A PIECED CRAZY QUILT RUNNER

I made my runner 12" x 30", which fits my table. Adjust the dimensions for use on your own table. You will need to strip piece your fabrics to get the desired background size.

Materials:
- Background of strip pieced fabrics – 12" x 30" or customized size
- Batting (optional)
- 14" x 32" piece of cotton print for backing and binding
- Assorted silk ribbons:
  Many colors – choose multi-colored or stay in one or two color families to blend with your decor
- Silk threads in several colors to match the ribbons and others to embellish

To piece the runner, use your favorite method of crazy or foundation piecing, or try my informal strip piecing method. To do this, begin with three or four straight-edged scraps sewn together on the machine. Then with a rotary cutter, cut through the scraps at an angle, turn them around, and sew them together again on a different edge.

Continue to add straight-edged scraps to the piece on all sides. Then cut, turn, and sew it together again. If an edge becomes ragged, cut a new edge. Repeat, making blocks which can be trimmed and sewn together, or keep going until you have a 12" x 30" (or customized size) runner top.

Next, put the runner on your hoop and begin embellishing it. Your embroidery guide will be the seam lines of your strip piecing. Each seam should be covered or outlined with stitching. You can embroider in the centers of the pieces as well. This is a good time to try some of the combination stitches, especially the fans and medallions or just be creative using stitches from the stitch chapter. Plan to do lots of combining of silk ribbon and thread. Some possible choices are on the next page. Use your imagination. Put your background fabric into the hoop and begin.

When you have finished embellishing the runner, take it off the hoop. Trim the edges if needed. Lay it on top of the batting (optional) and backing. Do simple outline quilting around the major pieces, but do not quilt on the silk ribbon areas. Bind by bringing the backing over the front and blind-stitching down.

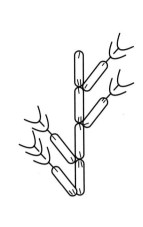

Ribbon feather stitching
Thread fly stitches on top

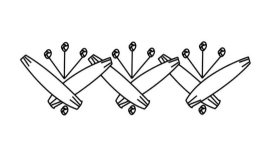

Ribbon cross-stitch
Thread pistil stitch
Ribbon French knots

Ribbon lazy daisy
Thread stem
Ribbon stitch leaves

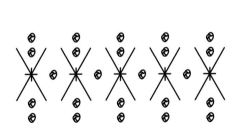

Thread cross stitch
Couched with contrasting thread
Ribbon French knots

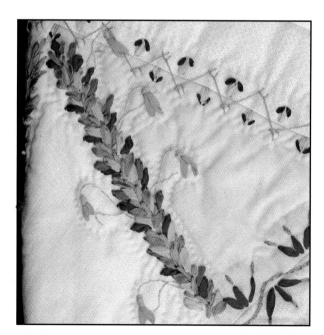

Crazy quilt runner details. Cathy Grafton.

ABOVE: Family crest. Cathy Grafton.
BELOW: Family crest detail.

FAMILY CREST
Grafton Family

On a trip to England my daughter Sarah put her money into a genealogy machine and got a complete printout of the history of the Grafton family. It was great fun for all of us to read and I was especially intrigued by the Latin motto – "et decus et pretium vecti." It means "both the glory and reward of integrity," which sounded like a pretty good motto to me. I decided to make a family crest. You can make one too!

I used some beautiful white Chinese silk thread for the Latin lettering. The stitches are worked on silk noil (commonly called raw silk) and I used some silk leaf for the batting. If you look at the designs, you will see that they are nothing more than elaborate strands which by now you should be able to make quite well if you have been practicing all along.

MAKING A FAMILY CREST

You may need to do a little genealogy research on this one if you wish to include a Latin motto. If you don't have a motto, perhaps you have a favorite family expression you can use instead. You will also need to choose a lettering style. I used an old English style since that is our background. A calligraphy book will give you some possibilities or you can use simple block printing. I outlined the letters in the name with silk thread and filled them in with a four-strand floss silk using a split stitch, an excellent filler stitch. Silk thread used to fill these letters creates a very effective luster. If you cannot find a multi-strand floss, use silk twist and work it with a stem stitch if it has too much twist to easily work a split stitch.

Materials:
- 15" x 22" piece of silk noil (raw silk), linen or muslin. To make your flowers glow, consider using a medium or dark colored background.
- 16" x 23" piece of batting
- 16" x 23" piece of print fabric for backing
- Assorted silk ribbons:
    three greens to build your strands
    lots of flower colors and shaded ribbons
- Silk thread
    one color for outlining the letters of the name
    one color for outlining the letters of the motto or saying
    several colors to fill in the lettering floss silk, if possible
    several greens for stems
    accent colors for feather stitching

On your background fabric, lightly pencil in the lettering of your last name just above the mid-line of your fabric. Below your name, pencil in the motto or saying you will be using. A light colored chalk pencil works well on darker fabrics.

Put the fabric in your hoop and stitch the lettering of your name with silk thread using a stem stitch. Fill in each letter with silk thread using either the split stitch or a stem stitch. Next stitch your motto using a stem stitch. French knots are a great way to dot the "i's."

You will build strands in two areas (see photo for placement). Build the three upper strands using the green silk ribbon, twining it with the first letter of your name, but being careful not to obscure the lettering. Add a few flowers to the strand using flower colors and the detached twisted chain stitch. Embellish this strand with lots of small spider web roses. Use several colors or shaded ribbon. Decorate the roses with fine silk threads worked in feather stitching. To further embellish this strand, work some pistil stitches with silk thread.

The lower strand will twine with the right end of your motto lettering. Again, be careful not to let the strand obscure the lettering. After working the strand with your green silk ribbon colors, add a few flowers using the detached twisted chain stitch. Embellish this strand with hanging flowers, grape clusters, and ribbon stitch branches. The grapes should nestle right up against the strand in several places. Use shaded ribbons or three shades of purple silk ribbon for the grapes. See Chapter 5 for tips on embroidering grapes.

Make the hanging flowers with three filled lazy daisy stitches using two colors. Attach them to the strand with silk thread and don't forget a stitch or two to form a calyx.

Finally, make the ribbon stitch branches by working some silk thread lines out from the strand using a stem stitch. Along one side of each of these branches work a row of ribbon stitches using silk ribbon. To further embellish this strand, fill in with single feather stitching done in silk thread.

Remove the hoop and mark a simple angled quilting design. I suggest triple rows spaced ¼" apart and grouped every 1" to 1½". Assemble with the batting and backing and quilt.

To finish your crest, bind by bringing the backing fabric over the front and blind stitching it down. Use the invisible wire method (page 105) for hanging, if desired.

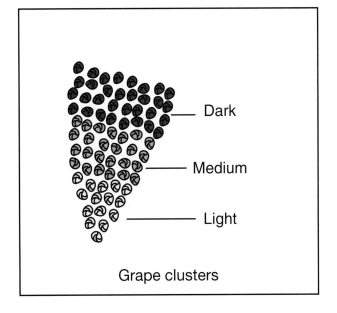

Grape clusters

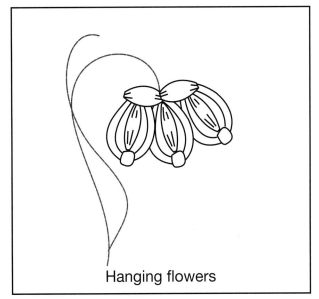

Hanging flowers

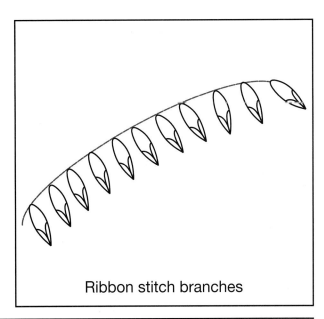

Ribbon stitch branches

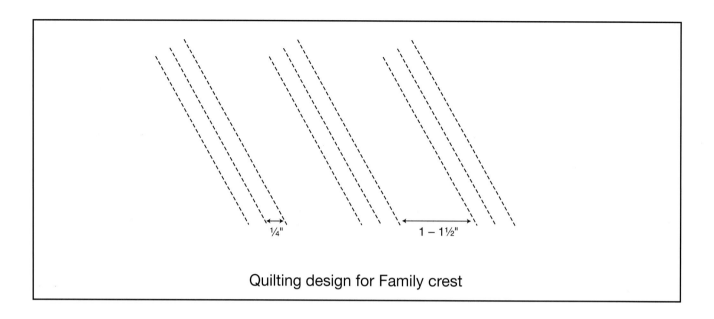

Quilting design for Family crest

¼"   1 – 1½"

Family crest detail.

ABOVE: Dave and Omi's Huis. Cathy Grafton.
BELOW: Dave and Omi's Huis detail.

CELEBRATION
Dave and Omi's Huis

My brother recently married and his wife Naomi is of Dutch descent. I wanted to make them a silk ribbon piece to celebrate their marriage and the purchase of their first home. In Dutch, house is "huis," so this became the message on their small sampler. I like the idea of centering the writing within an oval shape for this piece. I borrowed the idea of a bow with three loops, which I thought appropriate for newlyweds, from Baltimore album quilts.

MAKING A
CELEBRATION SAMPLER

You can adapt this design for newlyweds, anniversaries, new babies or to commemorate any special event. The oval is a secondary design and a working base.

Materials:
- 10" x 10" piece of linen or muslin for top
- ¼ yard of print fabric for border
- 16" x 16" piece of print or striped fabric for backing
- 16" x 16" piece of batting
- Assorted silk ribbons:
  multiple flower colors (at least 10)
  medium green – 7 mm to outline oval
- Silk thread for lettering, stems and decorative stitching (6 – 8 colors)

On your background fabric, mark a 9" x 9" square. With a pencil mark the oval shape in the center of the muslin. Lightly write in names and a central word or phrase (see illustration for placement). If desired, leave space along the inside bottom of the oval to add a couched silk ribbon bow.

Put the fabric in your hoop and stitch the letters with silk thread using a stem stitch. Use fairly strong colors to make the words stand out. Next, with the green 7 mm silk ribbon, outline the oval using a stem stitch.

The oval now becomes your working base. On the top half of the oval work small flowers – tiny spider web roses, fly stitch flowers, and ferns. Look in the combination stitch section and at the detail of this sampler for other ideas. Use both silk ribbon and silk thread in your flowers. Fill in the area until you have a pleasing design. You may repeat some of the flowers or do each one differently. Strive for color variety as well. After making all the flowers, add single feather stitching with silk thread if there are some spaces to fill.

On the bottom half of the oval, you will be working on a more uniform design. With silk thread, work alternating feather stitches in the same color all the way around the bottom of the oval. Top each of these with silk ribbon French knots. Go over the same area one more time with another color of silk thread, this time working ferns with single feather stitching for contrast.

If you are adding a couched bow, choose a silk ribbon accent color and tie a bow knot or make a three loop bow and pin it just inside the oval along the bottom. Beginning with one loop, couch it down with French knots in a matching color of thread. Complete all the loops and then couch down the ends. Remember to twist the ribbon after every one or two stitches and change direction often to get a flowing effect.

To finish this sampler, remove the hoop and trim your square. Next, cut the border fabric in three inch strips and sew them onto the four sides of the square. Mark a ¾" quilting grid outside the oval on the background fabric using a chalk pencil. Inside the oval you can do simple outline quilting ¼" from the lettering and bow. If you are using a print fabric with a regular pattern on the border, try quilting along the lines in the pattern. Otherwise, mark a quilting design of your choice.

Add your batting and backing and quilt the piece. Then bring the back over the front to bind the edges, and use the invisible wire method (page 105) to hang the quilt. Finish with a line of quilting just inside the binding.

Placement diagram

Appliqué Sampler

Shaker Wreath. Cathy Grafton.

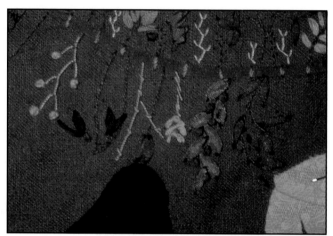

Shaker Wreath detail.

Shaker Wreath detail.

Wreath of flowers drawing.
Hancock Shaker Village, Pittsfield, Massachusetts.

APPLIQUÉ SAMPLER –
Shaker Wreath

The Shakers were a communal religious group that practiced celibacy and productive labor, and were dedicated to a life of perfection. Today they are best known for their excellence of workmanship in furniture and handicrafts. One of their maxims is "Hands to work and hearts to God." Some of their religious expression comes down to us in the form of Shaker spirit drawings which were created by brothers and sisters at the Pittsfield, Massachusetts, Hancock village during a time of religious fervor. Each drawing conveyed great symbolism and spiritual meaning.

One of my favorite Shaker spirit drawings is a watercolor of a wreath lined on both sides with flowers. This drawing inspired my Shaker wreath appliqué sampler. It is a combination of silk ribbon and appliqué flowers, joined together with a couched circle of ribbon. Because this is a complicated sampler, I suggest you try it only after you are fairly comfortable using the ribbon and working the stitches.

MAKING A SHAKER WREATH

Although this wreath looks complicated, it was built up layer by layer, similar to building a strand. The only pre-marked part is the circle! With a few appliquéd flowers and lots of silk ribbon, you can create your own version of this wreath. Although it looks as if there is random placement of the flowers, repetition of color, and stitching tie the piece together.

On your background fabric, lightly pencil a circle 8" in diameter. You will work on both sides of this circle, one side at a time. The scale of the flowers and other designs on the inside of the circle will be somewhat smaller than those on the outside of the circle.

Materials:
- 18" x 18" piece of silk noil (raw silk) linen or muslin. Consider using a medium background color which will allow you to use more white and cream colored ribbons and threads.
- Mottled or print fabric scraps for appliqué flowers
- 19" x 19" piece of batting
- 19" x 19" piece of cotton print for backing
- Assorted silk ribbons:
    a principal green for the circle and to use throughout the piece to create a feeling of unity
    several secondary greens for contrast
    all the flower and accent colors you have available
    shaded ribbons
- Silk thread
    to match the principal green color
    some secondary greens
    accent colors including some white or cream

Begin by threading a needle with a gray or lighter green silk thread. Take your principal green silk ribbon and shape it around the circle, pinning it in a few places. Couch over it every ¼" with silk thread, keeping the ribbon from twisting. Do this without a hoop so that you do not have to continually reposition the fabric. Do not pull the couching thread too tightly because you want the ribbon to lay flat without looking puckered. When you have gone all the way around the circle, slip a needle onto the end of the ribbon and gently stitch through to the back and tie off the ribbon. Then cover this spot with a couched thread stitch. Since your circle is couched down, not sewn down, you must be somewhat careful not to pull it or it might snag before you complete the next step.

Position your fabric on the hoop and thread your needle with the green silk thread that matches

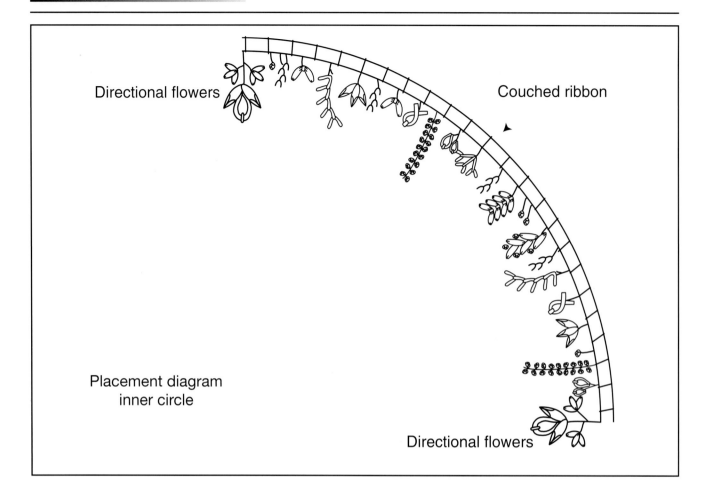

Directional flowers

Couched ribbon

Placement diagram
inner circle

Directional flowers

the circle ribbon. Go around the inside of the circle making small stems (4 to 6 stitches) using a stem stitch. Let some of these stems curve slightly and give others a side stem. They should be spaced about ¼" to ½" apart. At each of the four quarters of the circle, make a slightly longer stem. These will be directional flowers to add continuity to the piece. As you make these stems, let some of them just catch the edge of the couched silk ribbon circle. This will help secure it and keep it from pulling out of shape.

You now have a couched circle of silk ribbon with a lot of little stems to decorate. Top each of these stems with some type of silk ribbon flower. They can be very simple ones, adding just a touch of color. Begin with the four longer directional stems. These can be topped with a ribbon lazy daisy – I chose four related but different colors. Then using the matching principal green ribbon, form a calyx and several leaves along the stem.

With one of your silk ribbon flower colors, begin to make flowers on the different stems. To space your colors, make one or two flowers of the same color in each quarter section of the circle. Suggested stitches are the fly stitch, three ribbon stitch petals, French knots, small lazy daisy stitches, and single feather stitches. See some examples above. Try to vary the stitches as you go, using a good variety of colors and shades of the same color.

When you have topped each stem with a small stitched flower of some sort, you are ready to add some silk thread embellishment to the inner circle. Choose two colors of fine silk thread – one dark and one light. With the lighter color, work some tiny alternate feather stitching ferns between the flowers. Don't place them between each flower, but space them fairly regularly around the circle to give a sense of regularity to the inner circle. With the dark silk thread, do the

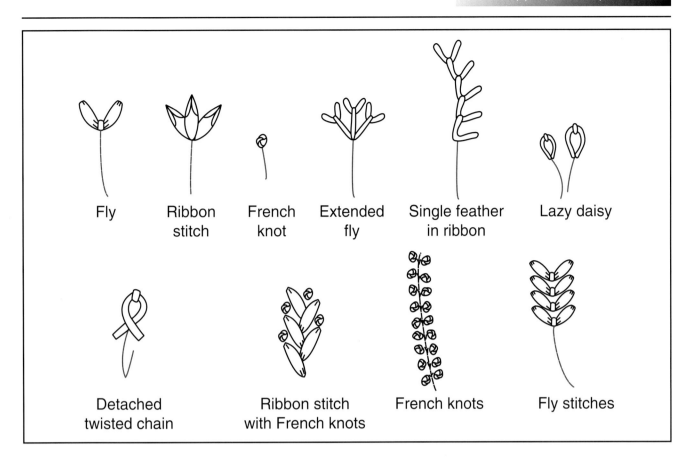

Fly

Ribbon stitch

French knot

Extended fly

Single feather in ribbon

Lazy daisy

Detached twisted chain

Ribbon stitch with French knots

French knots

Fly stitches

same thing, using the single feather stitch to fill in any spaces so that your flowers and embellishments almost touch all the way around the inside of the circle. To finish the inside of the circle, take a strong accent color of silk ribbon and work an eight-pointed star in the center using the ribbon stitch.

Now you are ready to work on the outside of the circle. This will be a three step process. First make stems much as you did on the inner circle. Second, add the ribbon flowers on top of these stems. Finally, finish with the appliqué flowers.

Work on the outer circle much as you did on the inner one. Remember, these flowers are worked on a somewhat larger scale than those on the inside of the circle. Position your hoop on the fabric and with the principal green silk thread, make the four directional stems first. These stems should look as if the inner stems had carried

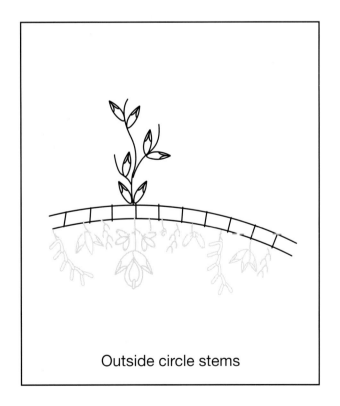

Outside circle stems

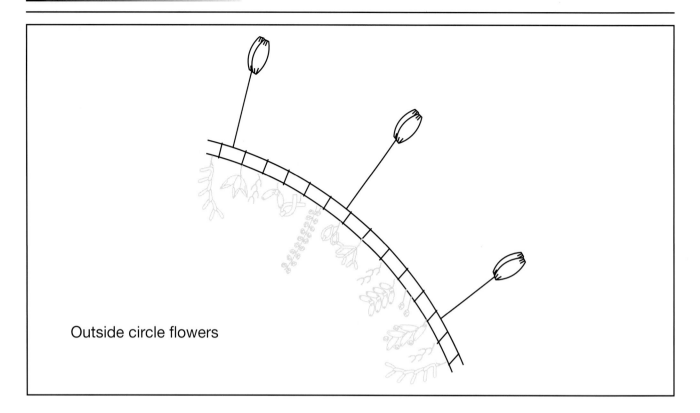

Outside circle flowers

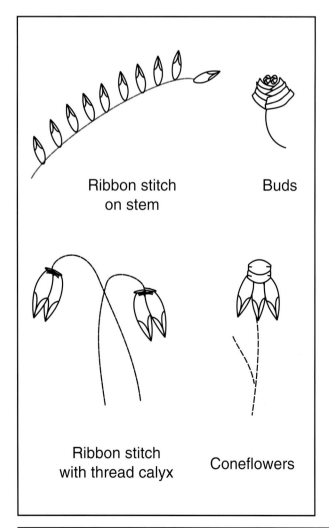

Ribbon stitch
on stem

Buds

Ribbon stitch
with thread calyx

Coneflowers

through, and they should curve and have a side stem. As you finish each of these stems, add a few ribbon stitch leaves with the principal green silk ribbon. Leave these until the third step when they will be topped with appliqué flowers.

Between these curved stems in each quarter of the outer circle, work three or four straight stems using the same green thread and the stem stitch. Top each of these straight stems with two straight stitches to form a calyx using the principal green ribbon. These also will be topped later with appliqué flowers.

Now using other green silk thread, make stems in the remaining spaces, again using the stem stitch. Try making some of these stems in small groups and somewhat curved. However, do not work them quite as closely as you did on the inner circle. Leave a little space between them for some ribbon flowers. Again for continuity, create some regularly placed stems, this time using the alternate feather stitch. Top each hook all the way around the circle with silk ribbon French knots worked with the same color of silk.

Petals for
directional flowers

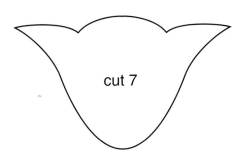

Fantasy flower #1

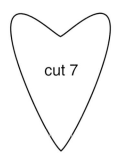

Fantasy flower #2

Add seam allowances for appliqué

Now you are ready to go back over the stems with different colors of ribbon to give them flowers. Again, be creative with the stitches and colors for the best affect. For some examples of flowers, see the illustration on page 128.

Look through the combination stitch section for other ideas, or try some of your own.

When you have filled up the outer circle with ribbon flowers, you are ready to remove the piece from the hoop and add the appliqué flowers to those stems reserved for them. There are three types of appliqué flowers to add. Use the shapes at left or design your own. Choose one color of fabric for each flower shape. You will need these pieces for the appliqué flowers:

Petals for directional flowers (cut 12)
Fantasy flower #1 (cut 7)
Fantasy flower #2 (cut 7)

The first flowers to position and blindstitch down are the directional petals. These go on top of the curved directional stems that divide the circle into quarters. Use two petals for the top flower and one for a bud on each side stem. Because these go on curved stems, each will be a little different in placement. You may want to add a calyx to them with silk ribbon after they are sewn down.

Fantasy flowers #1 and #2 will alternate around the circle on the straight stems. These flowers help keep the viewer's eye moving around the circle.

The original drawing has a simple blue border. Add a border if you like. Choose a backing that compliments the front colors – perhaps a dark print. Lay the piece on top of the batting and backing. Do outline quilting around the shapes. This is not a piece that needs lots of quilting. Bring the back over the front for a simple touch of color in the binding and use the invisible wire method (page 105) to stiffen the piece for hanging.

Appliqué Quilt

Wildflower Basket. Cathy Grafton.

Wildflower Basket details.

APPLIQUÉ QUILT or WALLHANGING
Wildflower Basket

This block design features a fabric basket, appliqué flowers and stems, silk ribbon and silk thread embellishments, and three strands of silk ribbon for filler. The flower designs are repeated in the border. It is shown here as a single block with borders which makes a 30" sampler or wallhanging.

This design could be increased to four blocks to make a small wall quilt or you could add more blocks for a full-size bed quilt.

The appliqué work here is very simple to allow for practice in combining fabric and silk ribbon. Use the illustrated placement as a guide, but feel free to try flowers in other positions as well. Appliqué by hand or machine, as you prefer. I use needle-turn appliqué with a scant ⅛" seam allowance.

MAKING A WILDFLOWER BASKET

Your choice of print for the basket is important to the overall look of this quilt. You will use it again on the outer border, so the colors in it will give you a base for the silk ribbon colors. I have chosen a Smithsonian print, but for a country look, plaid would be great, or consider a geometric print for a more cosmopolitan look.

Template patterns are given on pages 134 and 135 for the appliqué pieces – basket, flowers, petals, and leaves. The fabric stems are made from ¾" strips of leaf fabric cut on the bias.

Materials:
- ⅝ yard muslin square for the second border
- 1 yard of print material for basket and outer border
- 1½ yards of accent print for inner border, backing and binding
- Assorted colorful fabric scraps for flowers
- 32" x 32" piece of batting
- Green, gray, brown, or gold scraps for stems and leaves
- Assorted silk ribbons:
    at least three greens for leaves and strand
    several flower colors
- Silk thread for grasses, stems, and decorative feather stitching

Begin by cutting out your fabric basket. Then cut a 12½" x 12½" muslin square and lightly crease it in half to find the middle. Place your fabric basket centered on the lower half of the block and stitch it down.

At this point, add the first border which serves as a frame. Cut 2" strips of the accent fabric and sew to all four sides of the block.

Now you will build three strands with silk ribbon (see pages 138 – 139 for placement). Use three leaf colors – green, gold, or gray. Finish off each strand off with an embellishment of silk thread in an alternating feather stitch, if desired.

FOLDED FABRIC STEMS

Now work your fabric stems (see pages 136 – 137 for placement). Use a ¾" piece of bias fabric in the same color you plan to use for the leaves. Iron the strip in half lengthwise. Pin it to the block in the curved position. With a running stitch close to the raw edge, sew the strip to the background. Remove pins, turn the folded edge over, covering the raw edge, and blindstitch it down. This will give you a finished stem a little less than ¼" wide.

APPLIQUÉ FLOWERS AND LEAVES

Cut out your flowers and leaves from the fabric scraps. The number of pieces needed is given on the pattern. If you are making more than one block, multiply accordingly.

Begin with placement of the petals of the central flower. This will be a focal point of the block, so choose a strong color. Place the petals on the top line of the basket, just to the right of center (see page 137), and sew them down. The circles are yo-yos. Cut them out, gather the edges and tie off the thread to make finished yo-yo circles. Pin these circles to the left fabric stem along with the three leaves and stitch them down. Add the leaves to the fern stem and stitch them down. Note that some leaves extend into the border. Position these flowers. Stitch them down later after embroidering their stems.

SILK THREAD STEMS AND LEAVES

Position your hoop on the block and use the stem stitch to form the left and right stems coming out of the basket. You want these flowers to extend down from the basket. Mark the stems lightly with pencil if you wish (see pages 138 – 139 for placement). Use green or brown silk thread in fairly dark shades so that they will stand out. Remove the hoop and finish stitching down the fabric flowers, letting them extend into the border.

Now reposition your hoop and add the leaves and calyxes to your flowers. Leaves can be done in the ribbon stitch (left side) and lazy daisy (right side). Also add some stamens to the left flowers with the pistil stitch.

SILK THREAD GRASSES AND EMBELLISHMENTS

Finish off the block by adding more touches of silk thread to the design. I have added fly stitch grasses to the side of the central flower, French knots in the center of the flower, and single feather stitching with silk thread between the petals. Other grasses are done with silk thread and a lazy daisy stitch ending with a stem stitch (see page 139). Fill in with baby's breath or grasses using silk thread and ribbon to add a few more touches of color.

If you are making a single block sampler, continue adding two more borders to frame your piece. Make the second border from 3" strips of the central block fabric and the final outer border from 5½" strips of the basket fabric.

BORDER DESIGNS

Now work some of the same flowers into two corners of the borders. If you are making a larger quilt, you might want to put them in each corner, but for the smaller design, two is plenty.

For the top border design, begin with your silk thread stems. Position your hoop and repeating the same colors of stems you used earlier, form stems that come one-third of the way down the left side and across the top. These stems should be mainly on the central block fabric, but may spill onto the other border fabrics. Be sure to make a few side stems as well. Now remove the hoop and appliqué the flowers onto the stems. Finish them off by adding silk ribbon leaves as you did on the block.

For the bottom border design, begin with the folded fabric stems. They also should extend about one-third of the way up the right side and across the bottom of the border. Cut and place leaves along the stems and stitch them down. Now add a few more yo-yo circles to repeat the flower design of the central block. Finish off the lower border with a few silk thread grasses, repeating the fly stitch and feather stitch in colors from the central block.

QUILTING AND BINDING

Lay the quilt top over the batting and backing. I suggest outline quilting around the flowers and leaves and quilting a 2" diagonal grid for the remainder of piece. Binding can be the same print as the inner border. Because this 30" x 30" piece is heavier than the other projects in this book, adding a fabric casing on the back for a hanging rod works better than the invisible wire method.

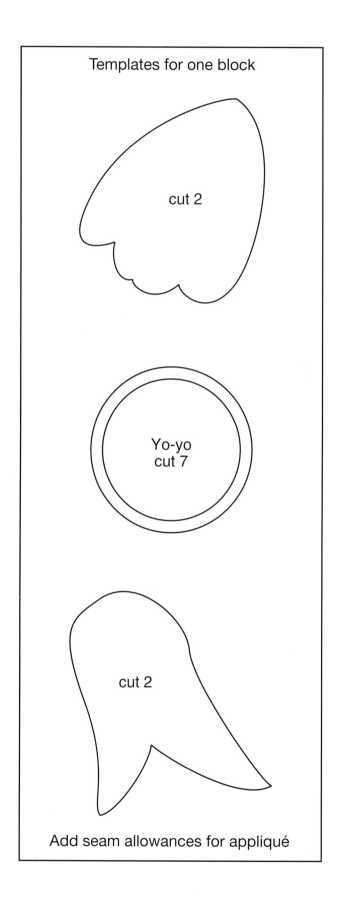

Templates for one block

cut 2

Yo-yo
cut 7

cut 2

Add seam allowances for appliqué

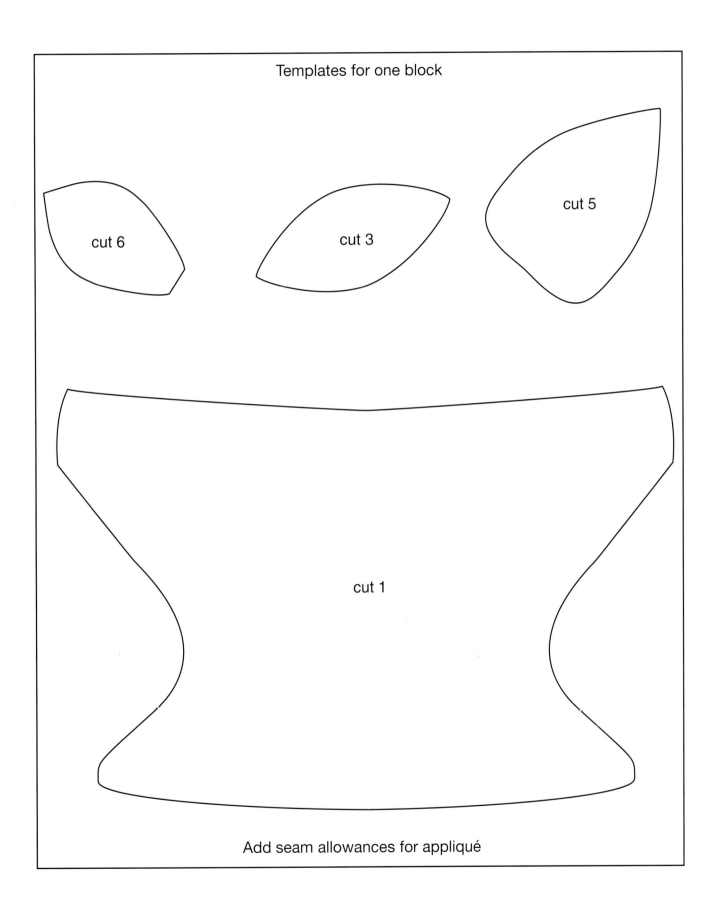

Templates for one block

cut 6

cut 3

cut 5

cut 1

Add seam allowances for appliqué

APPLIQUÉ PLACEMENT
for Wildflower Basket

Folded fabric stem

Gathered yo-yos

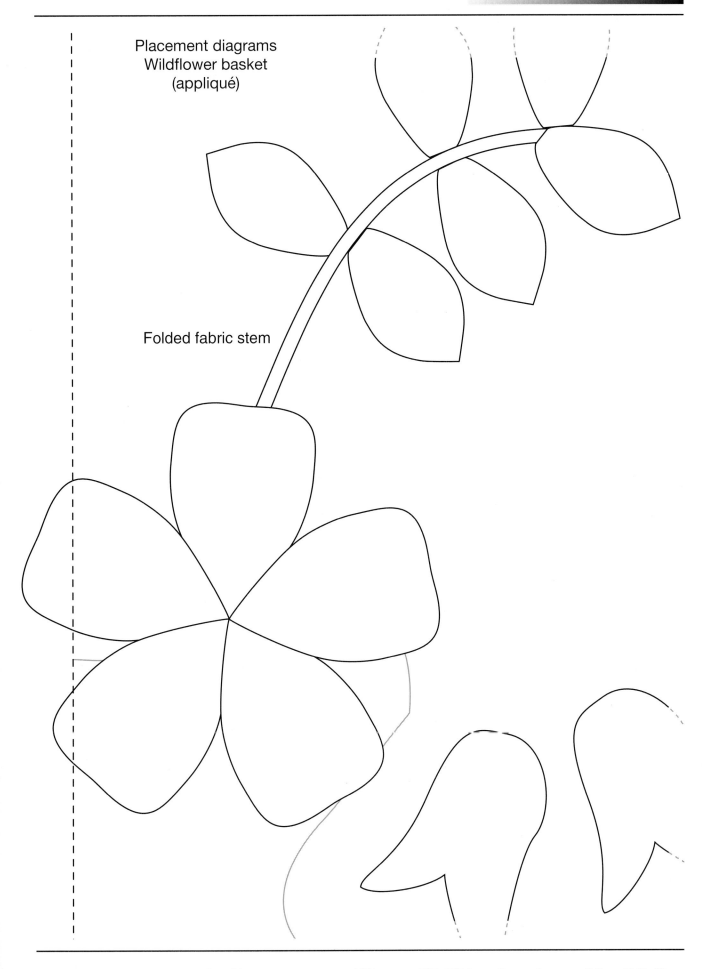

Placement diagrams
Wildflower basket
(appliqué)

Folded fabric stem

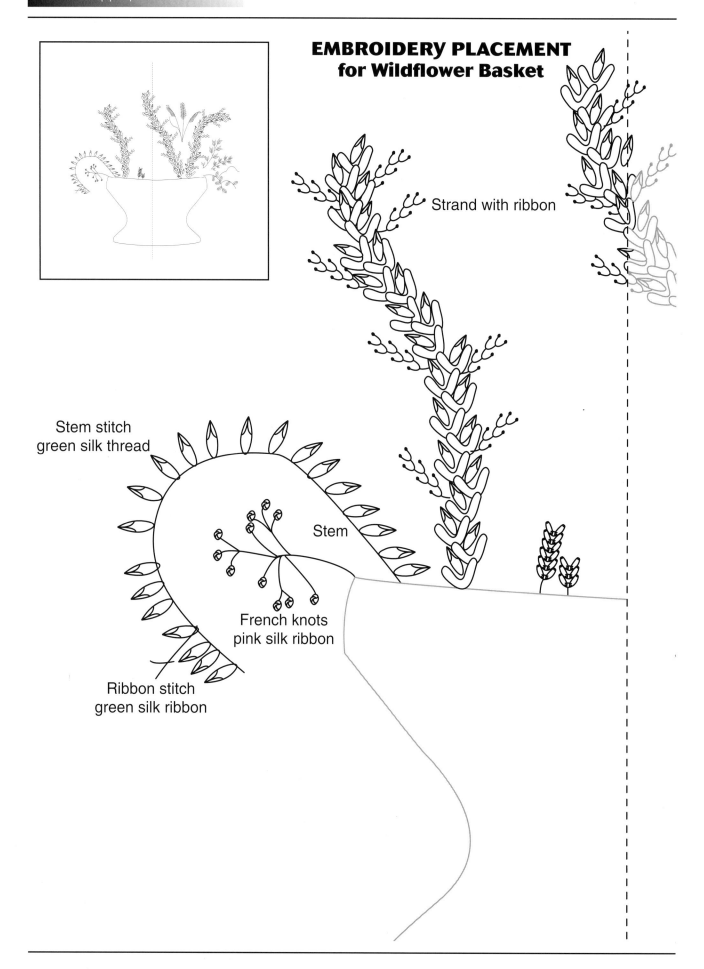

EMBROIDERY PLACEMENT
for Wildflower Basket

Strand with ribbon

Stem stitch
green silk thread

Stem

French knots
pink silk ribbon

Ribbon stitch
green silk ribbon

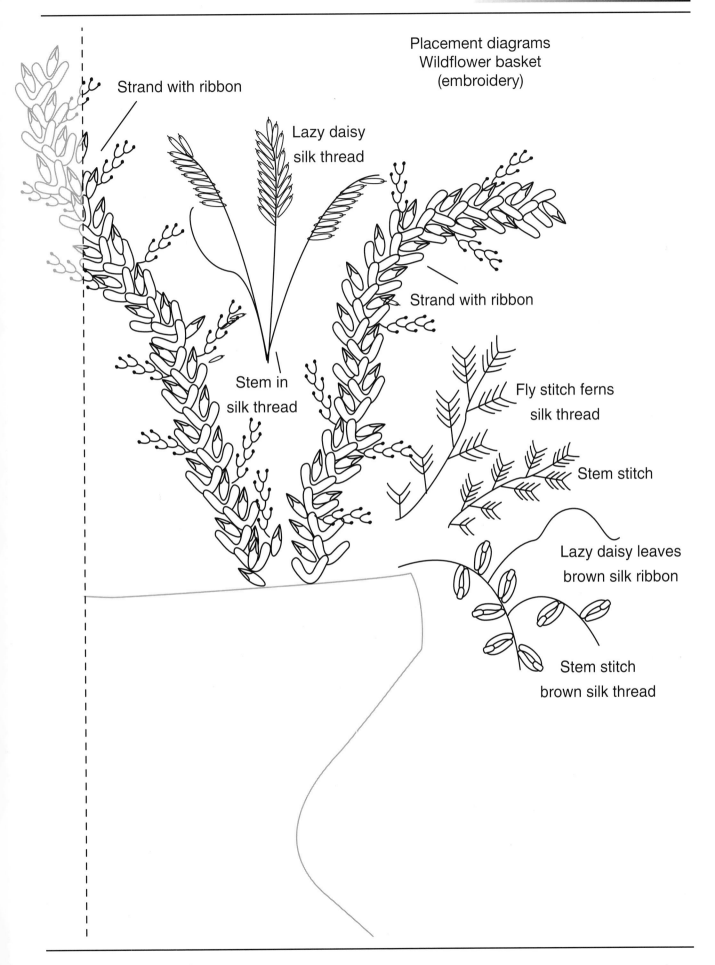

Placement diagrams
Wildflower basket
(embroidery)

Strand with ribbon

Lazy daisy
silk thread

Strand with ribbon

Stem in
silk thread

Fly stitch ferns
silk thread

Stem stitch

Lazy daisy leaves
brown silk ribbon

Stem stitch
brown silk thread

SOURCES AND SUPPLIES

Today it is much easier to find silk ribbon and threads. You may already know of several good sources in your area. Many quilt shops now carry a selection of ribbons and threads and will often special order colors if you ask them.

The following are some mail order sources which you may also want to use. Some of them are retail and some are wholesale. If your local shops do not yet carry silk ribbon, suggest some wholesale dealers and encourage them to order.

ANGELSEA

Retail – catalog $4.00
(partially refundable with order)
P.O. Box 4586
Stockton, CA 95204
209-948-8428
Silk ribbon, silk threads, metallic and hand dyed silk in dozens of colors. Lace and trim of all types and books. Contact Liz Dircksen.

DIVINE THREADS

Retail – mail order and at shows
321 E. Sloan Street
Mt. Vernon, MO 65712
417-466-3630
Silk ribbon, including over-dyed and edge-dyed types, threads, books. No minimum order.

ELSIE'S EXQUISITES

Retail and wholesale – catalog $5.00 (wholesale); retail info sheets are free
208 State Street
St. Joseph, MI 49085
800-742-SILK (orders)
616-982-0449 (other calls)
FAX: 616-982-0963
Silk ribbon and silk thread, European, vintage, reproduction and antique ribbons, patterns books and kits. Retail store open every day. Wholesale order minimum $100.00.

FRIENDSTITCH, LTD

Retail – catalog $2.00
4802 Rollingtop Rd.
Ellicott City, MD 21043
410-465-9645
Silk ribbon, silk thread, shaded ribbons, needles and notions. Specialize in threads of all types, books, hoops, and frames. Resident needlework designer and classes offered. Contact Pat or Margaret Fredinck.

LACIS

Retail and wholesale – catalog $5.00
3163 Adeline Street
Berkeley, CA 94703
510-843-7178
FAX 510-843-5018
Silk ribbon, silk thread, bias ribbon, other specialty threads. Pattern books, hoops and frames. Variegated bias cut ribbon in many colors.

POPLOLLIES & BELLIBONES

Wholesale only – write or call for samples
2700 11th Street Court
Moline, IL 61265
309-762-4951
Hand-dyed silk ribbon by Maureen Carlson.

QUILTERS' RESOURCE

Wholesale only
P.O. Box 148850
Chicago, IL 60614
312-278-5695
FAX: 312-278-1348
Silk ribbon, silk thread, specialty threads, shaded ribbons, needles, notions, and pattern books.

SHAY PENDRAY'S NEEDLE ARTS, INC

Retail – catalog $2.00
2211 Monroe
Dearborn, MI 48124
313-278-6266
FAX 313-278-9227
Silk ribbon, silk threads, flat silk, shaded ribbons, needles and notions, pattern books, hoops, and frames. They ship within 24 hours.

THINGS JAPANESE

Retail and wholesale – catalog $1.00
9805 NE 116th Street, Suite 7160
Kirkland, WA 98034
206-821-2287
FAX 206-821-2287
Silk ribbon, bias ribbon, silk thread, variety threads. "Dyeing in a teacup" kits, many dyeing supplies, and white silk for dyeing. Experts in all types of silk. Contact Maggie Backman.

WEB OF THREAD

Retail and wholesale – catalog is free
1410 Broadway
Paducah, KY 42001
800-955-8185 for charge card orders
502-554-8185
FAX 502-575-9700
Silk ribbon and variety of shaded ribbons, silk threads, and specialty threads. Needles, notions, patterns and books. Staff is knowledgeable. Same day shipping. Contact Sharee Dawn Roberts.

Dorothy Bond's book, CRAZY QUILT STITCHES

Available at quilting shops or order it directly from Dorothy ($12.00 + $3.00 shipping, 34706 Row River Rd. Cottage Grove, OR 97424). An excellent source of stitches and stitch combinations from old crazy quilts, many which could be done in silk ribbon. Clear illustrations, but little instruction.

BIBLIOGRAPHY

Beck, Thomasina. *The Embroiderer's Flowers*. Newton Abbott: David and Charles, England, 1993.

Bond, Dorothy. *Embroidery Stitches From Old American Quilts*. Dorothy Bond: Cottage Grove, OR, 1977.

Caulfield, S. F. A and Saward, Blanche. *Encyclopedia of Victoria Needlework*. Dover Publications, Inc.: New York, NY, 1972.

Daniel, Glenda. *Dune Country, A Hiker's Guide To The Indiana Dunes*. Swallow Press/Ohio University Press: Athens, OH, 1977.

Edwards, Betty. *Drawing From The Right Side of The Brain*. J. P. Tarcher, Inc.: Los Angeles, CA, 1979.

Eifers, Virginia S. *Flowers That Bloom in the Spring*. Illinois State Museum: Springfield, IL, 1970.

Enthoven, Jacqueline. *The Stitches of Creative Embroidery*. Reinhold Publishing Corp.: New York, NY, 1964.

Fallert, Caryl Bryer. *Caryl Bryer Fallert A Spectrum of Quilts 1983 – 1995*. American Quilters Society: Paducah, KY, 1996.

Krueger, Glee. *A Gallery of American Samplers*. E. P. Dutton/Museum of American Folk Art/ New York, NY, 1978.

Pye, David. *The Nature and Art of Workmanship*. Cambridge Univ. Press: Cambridge, Great Britain, 1968.

Reichel, William C. and Bigler, William H. *A History of the Rise, Progress and Present Condition of the Moravian Seminary For Young Ladies at Bethlehem, Pa., with its Catalogue of its Pupils*. 1785-1858. J. B. Lippincott: Philadelphia, PA, 1870.

Ring, Betty. *Girlhood Embroidery*. Alfred A. Knopf, Inc.: New York, NY, 1993.

Rogers, Gay Ann. *An Illustrated History of Needlework Tools*. Needlework, Unlimited, P.O. Box 181: Claremont, CA, 1983.

Saint, Aubin, Charles Germain de. *Art of The Embroiderer – 1770*. Los Angeles County Museum of Art/Trans.: Los Angeles, CA, 1983.

Schiffer, Margaret. *Historical Needlework of Pennsylvania*. Charles Scribners and Sons: New York, NY, 1968.

Fairbrother, Nan. *An English Year* (published in England under the name *Children in The House*). Alfred A. Knopf, Inc.: New York, NY, 1954.

Fields, Catherine K. and Kightlinger, Lisa C., eds. *To Ornament Their Minds: Sarah Pierce's Litchfield Female Academy 1792–1833*. Litchfield Historical Society: Litchfield, CT, 1993.

Groves, Sylvia. *The History of Needlework Tools and Accessories*. Newton Abbott: David and Charles, England, 1973.

Huish, Marcus B. *Samplers and Tapestry Embroideries*. Dover Publications, Inc.: New York, NY, 1963.

Johnson, Kathleen. *To Expand the Mind and Embellish Society*. Thesis. Winterthur, Museum Library: Winterthur, DE.

Knobel, Edward. *Field Guide to the Grasses, Sedges and Rushes*. Dover Publications, Inc.: New York, NY, 1980.

Kolander, Cheryl. *A Silk Worker's Notebook*. Interweave Press, Inc.: Loveland, CO, 1985.

Swan, Susan Burrows. *Plain and Fancy, American Women and Their Needlework, 1650 – 1850*. Holt, Rinehart and Winston: New York, NY, 1977.

Wheeler, Candace. *The Development of Embroidery in America*. Harper and Brothers: New York, NY, 1921.

Wright, Merideth. *Everyday Dress of Rural America, 1783 – 1800*. Dover Publications, Inc.: New York, NY, 1992.

ABOUT THE AUTHOR

Cathy Grafton is a midwestern quiltmaker who learned to love handwork at age seven. She began making quilts in 1971 and soon was teaching others. She participates in historical festivals as a demonstrating artisan and has designed her own quilts since 1981. She has taught and lectured extensively to quilt guilds and other groups throughout the Midwest.

Her ongoing work is a series of "prairie quilts" depicting the colors, farmland, and scattered images of the old prairie near her home. Her favorite design technique is free-cut appliqué in a folk art style. Since discovering silk ribbon embroidery, she has incorporated it into her quiltmaking.

She and her family live in Pontiac, Illinois, on the edge of the Grand Prairie.

AQS BOOKS ON QUILTS

This is only a partial listing of the books on quilts that are available from the American Quilter's Society. AQS books are known the world over for their timely topics, clear writing, beautiful color photographs, and accurate illustrations and patterns. Most of the following books are available from your local bookseller, quilt shop, or public library. If you are unable to locate certain titles in your area, you may order by mail from the AMERICAN QUILTER'S SOCIETY, P.O. Box 3290, Paducah, KY 42002-3290. Customers with Visa or MasterCard may phone in orders from 7:00–4:00 CST, Monday–Friday, Toll Free 1-800-626-5420. Add $2.00 for postage for the first book ordered and $0.40 for each additional book. Include item number, title, and price when ordering. Allow 14 to 21 days for delivery.

Item	Title	Price
4595	Above & Beyond Basics, Karen Kay Buckley	$18.95
2282	Adapting Architectural Details for Quilts, Carol Wagner	$12.95
1907	American Beauties: Rose & Tulip Quilts, Marston & Cunningham	$14.95
4543	American Quilt Blocks: 50 Patterns for 50 States, Beth Summers	$16.95
4696	Amish Kinder Komforts, Betty Havig	$14.95
2121	Appliqué Designs: My Mother Taught Me to Sew, Faye Anderson	$12.95
3790	Appliqué Patterns from Native American Beadwork Designs, Dr. Joyce Mori	$14.95
2122	The Art of Hand Appliqué, Laura Lee Fritz	$14.95
2099	Ask Helen: More About Quilting Designs, Helen Squire	$14.95
2207	Award-Winning Quilts: 1985-1987	$24.95
2354	Award-Winning Quilts: 1988-1989	$24.95
3425	Award-Winning Quilts: 1990-1991	$24.95
3791	Award-Winning Quilts: 1992-1993	$24.95
4593	Blossoms by the Sea: Making Ribbon Flowers for Quilts, Faye Labanaris	$24.95
4697	Caryl Bryer Fallert: A Spectrum of Quilts, 1983-1995, Caryl Bryer Fallert	$24.95
4626	Celtic Geometric Quilts, Camille Remme	$16.95
3926	Celtic Style Floral Appliqué, Scarlett Rose	$14.95
2208	Classic Basket Quilts, Elizabeth Porter & Marianne Fons	$16.95
2355	Creative Machine Art, Sharee Dawn Roberts	$24.95
4818	Dear Helen, Can You Tell Me? Helen Squire	$15.95
3870	Double Wedding Ring Quilts: New Quilts from an Old Favorite	$14.95
3399	Dye Painting! Ann Johnston	$19.95
2030	Dyeing & Overdyeing of Cotton Fabrics, Judy Mercer Tescher	$9.95
4814	Encyclopedia of Designs for Quilting, Phyllis D. Miller	$34.95
3468	Encyclopedia of Pieced Quilt Patterns, compiled by Barbara Brackman	$34.95
3846	Fabric Postcards, Judi Warren	$22.95
4594	Firm Foundations: Techniques & Quilt Blocks for Precision Piecing, Jane Hall & Dixie Haywood	$18.95
2356	Flavor Quilts for Kids to Make, Jennifer Amor	$12.95
2381	From Basics to Binding, Karen Kay Buckley	$16.95
4526	Gatherings: America's Quilt Heritage, Kathlyn F. Sullivan	$34.95
2097	Heirloom Miniatures, Tina M. Gravatt	$9.95
4628	Helen's Guide to quilting in the 21st century, Helen Squire	$16.95
2120	The Ins and Outs: Perfecting the Quilting Stitch, Patricia J. Morris	$9.95
1906	Irish Chain Quilts: A Workbook of Irish Chains, Joyce B. Peaden	$14.95
3784	Jacobean Appliqué: Book I, "Exotica," Patricia B. Campbell & Mimi Ayars, Ph.D	$18.95
4544	Jacobean Appliqué: Book II, "Romantica," Patricia B. Campbell & Mimi Ayars, Ph.D	$18.95
3904	The Judge's Task: How Award-Winning Quilts Are Selected, Patricia J. Morris	$19.95
4751	Liberated Quiltmaking, Gwen Marston	$24.95
4523	Log Cabin Quilts: New Quilts from an Old Favorite	$14.95
4545	Log Cabin with a Twist, Barbara T. Kaempfer	$18.95
4815	Love to Quilt: Bears, Bears, Bears, Karen Kay Buckley	$14.95
4833	Love to Quilt: Broderie Perse: The Elegant Quilt, Barbara W. Barber	$14.95
4598	Love to Quilt: Men's Vests, Alexandra Capadalis Dupré	$14.95
4816	Love to Quilt: Necktie Sampler Blocks, Janet B. Elwin	$14.95
4753	Love to Quilt: Penny Squares, Willa Baranowski	$12.95
2206	Marbling Fabrics for Quilts, Kathy Fawcett & Carol Shoaf	$12.95
4752	Miniature Quilts: Connecting New & Old Worlds, Tina M. Gravatt	$14.95
4514	Mola Techniques for Today's Quilters, Charlotte Patera	$18.95
3330	More Projects and Patterns: A Second Collection of Favorite Quilts, Judy Florence	$18.95
1981	Nancy Crow: Quilts and Influences, Nancy Crow	$29.95
3331	Nancy Crow: Work in Transition, Nancy Crow	$12.95
3332	New Jersey Quilts – 1777 to 1950: Contributions to an American Tradition, The Heritage Quilt Project of New Jersey	$29.95
3927	New Patterns from Old Architecture, Carol Wagner	$12.95
2153	No Dragons on My Quilt, Jean Ray Laury	$12.95
4627	Ohio Star Quilts: New Quilts from an Old Favorite	$16.95
3469	Old Favorites in Miniature, Tina Gravatt	$15.95
4515	Paint and Patches: Painting on Fabrics with Pigment, Vicki L. Johnson	$18.95
3333	A Patchwork of Pieces: An Anthology of Early Quilt Stories 1845 – 1940, complied by Cuesta Ray Benberry and Carol Pinney Crabb	$14.95
4513	Plaited Patchwork, Shari Cole	$19.95
3928	Precision Patchwork for Scrap Quilts, Jeannette Tousley Muir	$12.95
4779	Protecting Your Quilts: A Guide for Quilt Owners, Second Edition	$6.95
4542	A Quilted Christmas, edited by Bonnie Browning	$18.95
2380	Quilter's Registry, Lynne Fritz	$9.95
3467	Quilting Patterns from Native American Designs, Dr. Joyce Mori	$12.95
3470	Quilting with Style: Principles for Great Pattern Design, Marston & Cunningham	$24.95
2284	Quiltmaker's Guide: Basics & Beyond, Carol Doak	$19.95
2257	Quilts: The Permanent Collection – MAQS	$9.95
3793	Quilts: The Permanent Collection – MAQS Volume II	$9.95
3789	Roots, Feathers & Blooms: 4-Block Quilts, Their History & Patterns, Book I, Linda Carlson	$16.95
4512	Sampler Quilt Blocks from Native American Designs, Dr. Joyce Mori	$14.95
3796	Seasons of the Heart & Home: Quilts for a Winter's Day, Jan Patek	$18.95
3761	Seasons of the Heart & Home: Quilts for Summer Days, Jan Patek	$18.95
2357	Sensational Scrap Quilts, Darra Duffy Williamson	$24.95
3375	Show Me Helen...How to Use Quilting Designs, Helen Squire	$15.95
4783	Silk Ribbons by Machine, Jeanie Sexton	$15.95
1790	Somewhere in Between: Quilts and Quilters of Illinois, Rita Barrow Barber	$14.95
3794	Spike & Zola: Patterns Designed for Laughter...and Appliqué, Painting, or Stenciling, Donna French Collins	$9.95
3929	The Stori Book of Embellishing, Mary Stori	$16.95
3903	Straight Stitch Machine Appliqué, Letty Martin	$16.95
3792	Striplate Piecing: Piecing Circle Designs with Speed and Accuracy, Debra Wagner	$24.95
3930	Tessellations & Variations: Creating One-Patch and Two-Patch Quilts, Barbara Ann Caron	$14.95
3788	Three-Dimensional Appliqué and Embroidery Embellishment: Techniques for Today's Album Quilt, Anita Shackelford	$24.95
4596	Ties, Ties, Ties: Traditional Quilts from Neckties, Janet B. Elwin	$19.95
3931	Time-Span Quilts: New Quilts from Old Tops, Becky Herdle	$16.95
2029	A Treasury of Quilting Designs, Linda Goodmon Emery	$14.95
3847	Tricks with Chintz: Using Large Prints to Add New Magic to Traditional Quilt Blocks, Nancy S. Breland	$14.95
2286	Wonderful Wearables: A Celebration of Creative Clothing, Virginia Avery	$24.95
4812	Who's Who in American Quilting, edited by Bonnie Browning	$49.95